# THE PROFESSIONAL DESIGNER'S
## GUIDE TO
# MARKETING YOUR WORK

# THE PROFESSIONAL DESIGNER'S
## GUIDE TO
# MARKETING YOUR WORK

**MARY YEUNG**

NORTH LIGHT BOOKS

Cincinnati, Ohio

**The Professional Designer's Guide to Marketing Your Work.** Copyright © 1991 by Mary Yeung. Printed and bound in Hong Kong. All rights reserved. No part of this book may be reproduced in any form or by any electronic or mechanical means including information storage and retrieval systems without permission in writing from the publisher, except by a reviewer, who may quote brief passages in a review. Published by North Light Books, an imprint of F&W Publications, Inc., 1507 Dana Avenue, Cincinnati, Ohio, 45207. First edition.

95  94  93  92  91    5  4  3  2  1

Library of Congress Cataloging in Publication Data

Yeung, Mary
  The professional designer's guide to marketing your work / Mary Yeung.
    p.   cm.
  Includes index.
  ISBN 0-89134-368-7
  1. Graphic arts—United States—Marketing. 2. Design services—United States—Marketing. 3. Sales promotion. I. Title.
NC1001.6.Y48   1991
741.6'068'8—dc20

90-14190
CIP

Edited by Susan Conner
Designed by Clare Finney

*I want to thank all those who participated in this book. I especially want to thank my editor, Susan Conner, for all her suggestions and advice, and Nick DeBord, who taught me that a computer is my friend, not my enemy.*

# Contents

# *Introduction*

The dream of every graphic artist is to make a comfortable living doing the type of work he or she enjoys. This book is written especially for those artists who are thinking about breaking in to more lucrative markets, where the clients appreciate good work and are willing to pay a fair price for it. After all, if you have the talents and the skill, why should you have to supplement your illustration or design income by doing paste-up or selling art supplies? Why work for local businesses that can only afford to pay fifty dollars for a drawing, when you can earn thousands more doing similar work for upscale clients?

To compete on a higher level, you need direction from successful designers and illustrators who are already there. They'll advise you on how to attract, locate, and service clients with ample art budgets.

This book is divided into three parts. The first part provides you with vital information on how to build a more competitive portfolio, how to make a persuasive presentation, and how to find a good rep. We also take an inside look at how art directors hire illustrators and designers.

These chapters give you more than common-sense advice. They showcase current work from the portfolios of successful graphic designers and illustrators so you can examine the level of work you'll have to compete with.

The second part profiles ten young designers and illustrators who have built successful careers in graphic design and illustration. They are award-winning designers and illustrators who work for prestigious clients. These personal accounts of their career beginnings are honest and humorous, and they offer perceptive insights on how to deal with rejection, marketing, self-promotion, and collecting fees.

The third part of this book gives you the resources you'll need to survive and prosper in this competitive business. You'll find selected listings of important organizations, publications, advertising vehicles, and design competitions. I hope this book will help you get your foot in the right doors so you can earn a good living doing creative and challenging work.

Mary Yeung

# PROMOTING YOURSELF

Every day, thousands of illustration and design projects are being assigned to freelancers across America—book covers, theater posters, sales brochures, print ads, TV commercials, record album covers and magazine illustrations. The jobs are out there, waiting to be filled—all you have to do is find these clients and convince them you are the right person for the job.

Self-promotion is the art of letting the right people know that you have talent and that you're ready and available for assignments. That involves networking, cold calling, advertising, direct mailing, and building name recognition.

## NETWORKING

The day you decide to be an illustrator or graphic designer, you should announce it to the world: relatives, friends, neighbors, former employers, printers, and typesetters. Many jobs come from referrals, especially from fellow artists who are running into scheduling problems or who are offered jobs they don't feel are right for them. As a service to clients, they will suggest other illustrators or designers. The more established artists you know, the more referrals will come your way.

The best places to meet your peers are at professional functions, seminars, award dinners, and exhibits organized by design organizations in your hometown. In most cities, there are local chapters of the Art Directors Club, the American Institute of Graphic Arts (AIGA), and the Graphic Artists Guild.

Joining all these clubs would be costly, so choose those that can best serve your needs. It's difficult to recommend a particular organization, because the quality of each club varies from town to town, and from year to year, depending on the elected officers who are running it. However, you can do some investigating on your own by attending seminars and exhibits organized by these clubs. Most will admit nonmembers to their events, which may include major design conferences, educational seminars, parties, and lectures.

If your town doesn't have professional organizations for graphic artists, then join those located in a neighboring city or in major cities, such as New York, Chicago, or Los Angeles.

Be an active member. Go to the events and lectures to keep up-to-date on the industry. A lot of helpful gossip is exchanged at these functions. You might learn which art director is working on important projects, which printer is good and inexpensive, where to go for quality typesetting, or which clients don't pay their bills. Bring plenty of business cards with you, and exchange them whenever the appropriate opportunity arises. Building name recognition takes a lot of time and effort, but it pays off in the long run.

## COLD CALLS

If you're one of those artists who's afraid of making cold calls, you can take comfort in knowing that hundreds of artists have the same fear. It's natural to be nervous when you call a total stranger and ask him to look at your portfolio, but to be a successful freelancer, you must overcome this fear.

It's important to meet art directors and art buyers in person. In a face-to-face meeting, you get to sell your personality as well as your work. For example, if your work is good, *and* you seem like an easy person to work with, an art director may offer you a job on the spot. Even if there is no work available immediately, he or she can still keep you in mind for future projects.

A few years ago, it was much easier to get an appointment with an art director than it is today. There were fewer artists looking for work and fewer annuals, directories, and magazines available to help art directors keep up-to-date with upcoming young artists. But today, with so many publications servicing art directors, many directors have a policy of asking artists to simply drop off their books. However, this is not necessarily a dyed-in-the-wool policy. Very often, if you communicate how important it is for you to get their opinion about your work, they'll find the time to see you.

Set a goal for yourself to make at least three to five cold calls a day. When you call, keep these pointers in mind:

• Be persistent, but be patient and polite with the receptionist or secretary you're dealing with. If you sound annoyed or frustrated, you can be sure the boss will hear about that.

• If the art director is not in, leave a message with the secretary. Don't get discouraged if the art director doesn't return your call. You can always call back the next day. If you happen to call when she is in, she'll probably take the call. She understands that you have to make a living, too.

• Once you're on the phone with the art director, introduce yourself, briefly describe your work, and tell how your style might fit into the magazine or current design projects. Don't give a twenty-minute sales pitch on your work, and don't ask a million questions about the firm or the kind of project being worked on. Art directors are very busy people, and they don't have a lot of time to chat with every stranger who calls on the phone.

• If the art director tells you to drop off your portfolio, ask if he can find time to review the book with you. Say that you would value his feedback on your work.

• If the art director still insists that there is no time available to meet with you, don't argue. Just follow instructions and drop off your portfolio. Remember, persistence is admirable, but you don't want to get a reputation as being pushy.

## DIRECT MAIL PROMOTION

For many art directors, the most welcome form of self-promotion is direct mail. They get to see your work, but they don't have to spend time going through your portfolio explaining to you why they can't use your work. Believe it or not, it's just as painful to give rejections as it is to receive them.

For artists, direct mail is the least expensive and quickest way to get in touch with hundreds of potential clients. Try to create a promotional piece that can target different types of clients effectively. First determine the type of clients you want to work for, then design something that will be relevant to these clients' needs.

Generally, the piece you send should be the most outstanding piece in your portfolio. Send something that is memorable, yet applicable to commercial use. A reputable art director gets an average of ten to twenty promotional pieces from illustrators and designers a week, and most of them end up in the trash can. The reasons range from the wrong style to boring images, from unprofessional design to bad reproductions. You can't expect an art director to appreciate the beauty of your work when it is presented in an unprofessional manner, where too many images are cluttered together on a page, or when color pieces are poorly reproduced. Upscale clients expect to see high-quality promotional materials and will not entrust important projects to artists who create muddy looking, unappetizing mailings. They're not interested in your limited bank account; they just think you don't have high standards or that you are not trying hard enough.

Self-promotion is show biz. Make it dazzling, make it memorable. Even if the art directors can't use you this month, they'll still remember you're the designer or illustrator who sent them that great looking brochure. They'll remember your enthusiasm and your dedication to the craft. When one of their colleagues happens to be looking for an artist who works in your style, they'll remember your striking self-promotion piece, even though they've never met you in person.

Effective self-promotion doesn't have to break your bank. If you can't afford to spend ten thousand dollars on a twelve-page, four-color brochure, then come up with more intriguing concepts and designs that can be reproduced inexpensively, yet still show off your work beautifully.

On the whole, art directors appreciate work that is original and entertaining. So don't be afraid to take chances with your design and concept. As long as the piece is well executed and presented in a tasteful and sophisticated manner, you can send just about anything—a jar of peanut butter with a label you designed on it, a fan printed with your beautiful illustration, a humorous card announcing a move, a homemade Christmas card, and of course, the traditional brochures and mailers.

It is not necessary to include a résumé in your mailing, but you may wish to list some of your major clients in your postcards or brochures to show that you have professional experience. Or you can include an introductory letter that gives some background about your work experience and achievements.

If you wish to do something beautiful and elaborate but can't afford to do enough of it to send a mailing to two hundred people, then just send it to the people you're dying to work for. For example, if you're an illustrator whose work relies on brilliant color, but you can't afford four-color printing at this time, then consider printing up a small quantity using the Canon Laser Copier. One copy can cost anywhere from $2.50 to $6 depending on the copy shop you patronize. Make a list of your favorite art directors, people whom you really want to impress, and send them one of your beautifully printed illustrations as a promotional piece. Have it matted like a precious piece of artwork and wrap it up like a present. For the art director, it's a pleasant little surprise, a little extra effort that can make a memorable impression.

For art directors on the "B" list, select illustrations that rely more on design and concept, and send them good black-and-white reproductions instead.

## Upscale Clients

To establish yourself as an upscale designer or illustrator, you have to work for clients who will offer you the opportunity to do upscale projects, and you can find them in design and illustration annuals that showcase beautiful printed work, such as *Print Regional*, the *CA Advertising Annual*, and design annuals published by organizations like AIGA, the Society of Publication Designers, or the Type Directors Club. These publications showcase winning entries selected by a panel of prestigious judges (usually respected designers, art directors, and illustrators). The winning designs and illustrations are accompanied by captions that list the names of designers, illustrators, art directors, clients, and the cities in which the pieces were created. You can use this information to form a list of clients and art directors who you think might be interested in your style of work.

Promotional pieces for these clients should be beautifully designed and reproduced. The look should be tasteful, sophisticated, and refreshing. These clients are so accustomed to looking at the best that anything that looks amateurish is thrown out immediately.

## Special Industries

If you want to work for specific industries, mailing list companies like Creative Access and Steve Langerman are ready to help you. For instance, if you like to design brochures for furniture companies or hospitals, you can purchase mailing lists for these areas. Because art directors move faster than a speeding bullet, these lists are updated every three to four months. Prices vary from company to company, but the average rate is about ten cents a name with a minimum purchase of four hundred to five hundred names. These lists can be purchased in the form of computerized mailing lists, index cards, and mailing labels.

## Advertising Agencies

To get work from the advertising market, you can look through advertising annuals published by various design organizations for award-winning art directors. The One Club in New York City publishes an annual called *The One Show*. The Art Director's Club of New York and Los Angeles both publish their own annuals, and *Communication Arts (CA)* publishes the *CA Advertising Annual*, while *Print* publishes the *Ad-*

*vertising Case Book*. All these publications list clients, art directors, and agencies. These annuals will give you some idea which agency handles what accounts and the art directors that buy illustration.

Another valuable research source is *The Standard Directory of Advertising* and *The Standard Directory of Advertising Agencies*. They're often referred to as "Red Books" in the industry (because they have red covers). These directories cost about one hundred dollars each, so you might want to look for them in your local libraries.

*The Standard Directory of Advertising* lists thousands of large- and medium-sized corporations in the U.S. by alphabetical order and by product category. It tells you about the company's products or services, its media budget, and which advertising agencies it uses. This type of information can help you determine who the right clients are for you. For example, if the media budget for a particular company shows it spends 60 percent of its budget on TV commercials, 35 percent for radio, and 5 percent on print, this may not be a worthwhile company for you to pursue, since it obviously doesn't use a lot of print work.

*The Standard Directory of Advertising Agencies* lists large and small advertising agencies in the U.S. and their subsidiaries abroad. Listings include agencies' current clients, important creative directors, art directors, account executives, copywriters, and the agencies' addresses and phone numbers. However, it does not match the creatives with specific accounts, so you'll have to do a little investigative work. If you see an account you might like to work for, call the agency and ask for the art director for that account. You're not always going to get a lot of cooperation on the phone, since most receptionists at big agencies are not familiar with who works on what account, and in many cases staff members are not authorized to give you that information. But don't get discouraged; just be patient, polite, and persistent. If you ask enough times, you'll get the information you need.

Other helpful publications are *Adweek* and *Ad Age*. *Ad Age* publishes an annual that lists the one hundred leading national advertisers. In that issue, it also lists the top twenty-five advertisers for outdoor, print, TV, and a variety of categories.

## PUBLIC RELATIONS FIRMS

Public relations firms often need designers and illustrators to work on projects, and there are several listings you can buy or look for in your city's public library, including *O'Dwyer's Directory of Public Relations Firms* and *O'Dwyer's Directory of Corporate Communications*. Both list individual companies in the public relations field, as well as staff names, the activities of two thousand companies and over three hundred trade associations. Another helpful publication is *The Public Relations Register*, published by the Public Relations Society of America, which lists society membership geographically.

## ADVERTISING YOUR WORK

An effective way to reach potential clients is to advertise in the national directories, such as the *Creative Black Book*, *American Showcase*, or local directories, either the ones in your hometown or the ones in major cities. In California, there is the *L.A. Work-Book*; in Massachusetts, the *Design Source*; and in Illinois, the *Chicago Talent Sourcebook*. Advertising in these directories can be expensive. The *Black Book* charges over $5,000 for a full-page ad, and over $3,000 for a black-and-white page, while *American Showcase* charges about $3,500 for a full-color page. However, many art directors consult these directories for specialized talent. For an established artist, it's worth the price, since a few high-paying assignments can offset the cost.

For artists who haven't been in the business very long, your money is better spent on direct mail, where you can target your clients more precisely. You can always advertise later, when you're ready to compete with the artists featured in these directories.

## COMPETITIONS

Annuals are by far the best place to advertise your work. The only problem is, you can't buy your way into these books. Annuals published by *CA* , *Print*, The Art Directors Club, and the AIGA all showcase work that has been selected by judges. Everybody is eligible to enter into these competitions by paying a small entry fee (anywhere from ten dollars to sixty dollars depending on the organization), but you'll get published only if you are selected by the judges. Most organizations will tell you that they've received forty thousand entries, and that less than 6 percent were selected by the judges. It's really not as competitive as it sounds. I've seen many of these competitions in progress, and I've found that about 80 percent of the entries are very dull work. So if you enter work that is beautiful, innovative, and interesting, you'll have a good shot at it. Each year, exciting new talent is discovered through these competitions.

If you haven't been lucky enough to design such a beautiful piece for a client, then design a great self-promotion piece. Most annuals accept printed self-promotional projects.

Winning a competition is no guarantee you will get work, but it does increase your chances of being discovered by clients who are looking for quality illustration. Design annuals are read by designers, art directors, and editors who are looking for creative new talent. They may decide that you are the next superstar in the design world.

## REACHING FOR FAME

How do people get to be famous in this business? For some, it's talent, luck, and timing. It happens when an artist develops a style that is just right for the moment, or when the design community agrees that a particular style is the look of the '80s or '90s and everybody wants to use it to jazz up their project. And that particular artist's name forever lives in design history books.

For every Milton Glaser there are dozens of respected designers who are recognized as the leaders in the profession, people who start the trends and set the creative standards for the business. They are the people who give this profession respectability and earning power. To get to this level, you need to

consistently produce exceptional work. After interviewing hundreds of successful designers, I've found that most have taken similar steps to reach the top:

• Start with classical training in design and art history.

• Set ambitious career goals early. Make an extra effort to attract high-profile clients by developing upscale promotional materials or volunteering your design services to nonprofit organizations that want great design, such as clubs, theaters, dance companies, and local museums. This will help you develop a collection of beautiful tearsheets early in your career.

• Join prestigious design organizations, and become an active member. Get to know all the famous and would-be-famous designers and illustrators.

• Enter your creative work in all the important competitions and hope that your work gets selected by the judges and gets published in the annuals.

• Once you have a sizeable and impressive collection of published work, write letters to editors of trade magazines and tell them about yourself, the awards that you have won, and current exciting projects. Send them several samples of your best work.

• Put all the trade magazines on your mailing list and send them promos to keep them up-to-date on your latest developments. Editors are always looking for sources for their stories. If you give great quotes they'll call you over and over again and ask you to comment on all kinds of subjects. Before you know it, you could become a familiar name in the industry, and you'll be asked to give lectures, judge shows, and write books.

In the next few pages, you'll see some examples of self-promotion projects by young artists. Many of these projects didn't cost a lot of money to produce, but they are effective because the concepts are clever, the pages are well designed, and they leave you with a memorable concept or image.

# *Effective Self-Promotion*

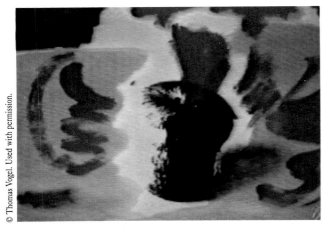

If you're a designer who wishes to work in the electronic media, you can show off your creative skills with a video project. A few years ago, Thomas Vogel, a young German designer, flew to New York to pick up a bronze award for his homemade music video from The International TV and Film Festival of New York. While he was in town, he decided to show his video to several design firms, including R/Greenberg (famous for computer animating, corporate logos and movie titles) and

Broadcast Arts, and also to visit creative director George Lois of Lois Pitts Gershon Pon/GGK, an advertising agency.

Although Vogel didn't have anything else to show because he had left his print portfolio in Germany, Lois was so impressed with the video that he hired Vogel as an art director. Today, Vogel owns his own design firm called Communication House in New York.

The music video, "Touch Me," was intended to be a self-promotional vehicle. Vogel

wanted the three-minute, forty-second piece to demonstrate his talent as a filmmaker and a designer. Vogel did everything from concept to production. The project took him several months and cost four thousand dollars. The result of this ambitious and expensive effort was a silver prize from the National Audio-Visual Festival in Germany, a bronze prize from the International TV and Film Festival in New York, and, of course, an art directing job in America.

# Anne D. Bernstein
## (We know she can draw little faces)

## But Can She Draw...

☑ AN APPLE

☑ A NEW YEAR'S CHAMPAGNE TOAST

☑ A FROG

☑ AN ODD GUY EXERCISING

☑ A PIG IN A TOGA

☐ A PHOTO-REALIST PORTRAIT OF BUSH

☑ A FUR-LINED CUP AND SAUCER

☑ A MAN WITH HIS FINGER IN A TUBE

☑ SANTA CLAUS

☑ BASEBALL

☑ A MONSTER WITH A PLUNGER

☐ A TECHNICAL RENDERING OF A CAR ENGINE

FOR DRAWINGS OF LOTSA DIFFERENT STUFF: (718) 956·1978

Anne Bernstein's humorous black-and-white promotional flyer brings a big smile to art directors. An appropriate clever concept always leaves a memorable impression.

Here's one promotional piece few clients would have the heart to throw away. It's a playful flipbook by New York illustrator Victoria Kahn to announce her new address. The piece demonstrates her enthusiasm for her crafty collage illustrations and her conceptual ability. It measures 3½ × 3½ inches and has a total of thirty-six pages, which are bound by industrial-strength staples. Although the project was time consuming, it left a memorable impression with the client. However, clever promotional pieces like this should be backed up with samples of your illustrations or designs.

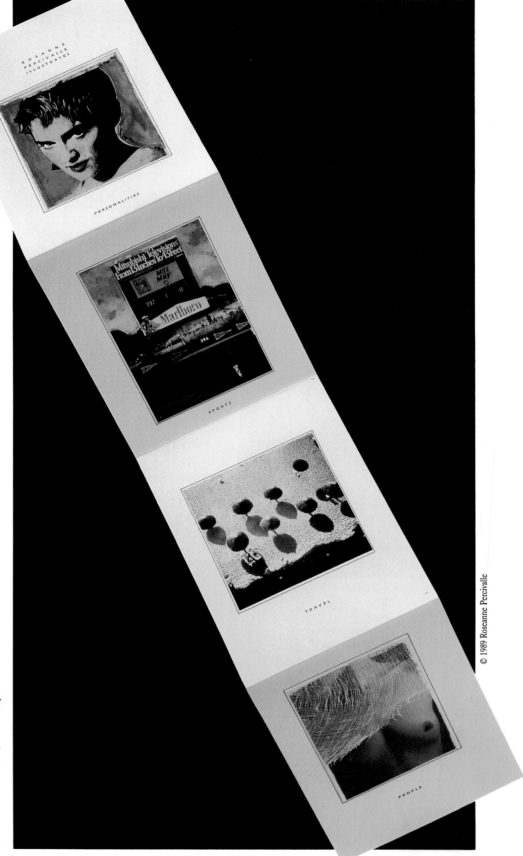

Rosanne Percivalle, an illustrator in New York City, created this impressive full-color, accordion-fold promo card. Instead of paying for expensive color separations, she printed art photo cards and pasted them on accordion folds printed with black type. The cost of using one-color printing and the photo cards was substantially less than paying for color separation and color printing, yet the result was just as effective.

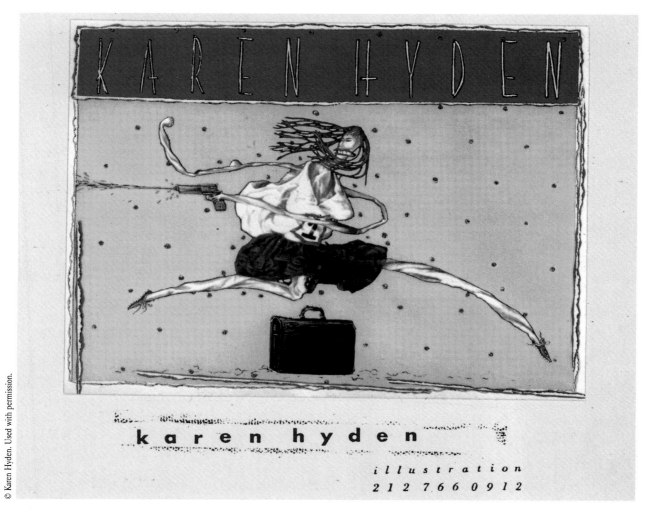

Karen Hyden, a young collage illustrator in New York City, created a charming, high-strung self-portrait and used it as a promotional piece. Hyden shot her illustrations on several rolls of low-speed 35mm film and had the film developed at a high-quality, one-hour photo lab. The resulting original photograph is sharper than copies. She mounted the photo on a gray card printed with her name and phone number. This method works well for Hyden only because she's a good photographer.

Hal Mayforth, an illustrator from Londonderry, New Hampshire, had many of his simple sketches made into rubber stamps. He has a rubber stamp for just about every occasion. The stamps are fun and entertaining, a friendly way to keep in touch with clients.

# Presenting Your Portfolio

With the advent of fax machines, computers, and overnight deliveries, today's illustrators and graphic designers are no longer at the mercy of local clients. Armed with a great portfolio, an illustrator living in a small town can work for metropolitan clients by using modern technology. On the other hand, innovative art directors no longer have to rely on local talent. Even with a low budget, they can hire talented young illustrators from other cities and towns. As a result of new technology, good artists will be discovered faster and get more assignments, while mediocre artists will have a harder time finding work because more competitive work is readily available. Today, if you don't have a first-rate portfolio, no amount of promotion and marketing efforts is going to help you get work.

## LEARN FROM THE BEST

Before revamping your portfolio, assess the quality of your work by comparing it with the best commercial artists in the country and not with the artists next door or the guy that did that cute little logo for Mrs. Bushwick's pastry shop down the block. You can find samples of good designs and illustrations in trade magazines like *Print*, *Graphis* and *Communication Arts* (*CA*). These magazines showcase work from the hottest graphic designers, illustrators, and photographers in the world. There are also annuals published by graphic arts organizations, such as the AIGA, the Art Directors Club, and the One Club (for advertising only), the Society of Illustration, and the Society of Publication Designers. The work in these annuals sets standards for the graphic design industry. Of course, the idea is not to imitate the styles and techniques featured in these publications, but to allow the quality of the work to inspire you to raise your own standard. Why be influenced by the artist who designed that tacky billboard on I-25 when you can learn from the best professionals in the field?

You should also solicit constructive criticism from respectable art directors from your own town, or in cities where you want to market your work. You may be too close to your own work to make an objective evaluation, undervaluing or overvaluing a particular piece or style. An objective, experienced eye can often point you in the right direction. Call several art directors on the phone and ask them to review your portfolio. Tell them how much you admire their work and that you would appreciate some helpful advice.

At this stage of the game, don't even attempt to second-guess the market. Just show your personal favorites—work that you would like to produce, not what you "think" will sell. People don't always know what they want until it's shown to them. Who could predict that punk fashion would captivate millions of young people, or that Andy Warhol's pop art style would influence a whole generation of artists? If your relatives shake their heads in puzzlement in response to your work, don't worry about it—they're not the authorities in the art field. Have a little faith in your own creations, and show your work to a few dozen art directors, and see if there is an audience for it.

If you suspect that your work is too sophisticated or too avant garde for the market in your hometown, don't be discouraged. Visit art directors in other cities where the market is more open to new ideas. Art directors of record album covers and lifestyle magazines, for example, are always complaining that they don't see enough innovative work. They believe too many young artists have stereotyped images of what's marketable. These art directors are always looking for fresh new styles to make their projects look current and exciting. In fact, many illustrators and designers who couldn't make a living in their hometowns have found financial and critical success in cities that are supposedly harder to compete in.

## MARKET ONE STYLE AT A TIME

To compete on a national level, you have to build name recognition by specializing in a particular area, such as portraits, nature illustrations, or technical drawings. Or you can market a signature style by creating a special "look" for all your drawings. This look must consistently convey a certain mood, i.e., "funky, fun, and youthful" or "moody and poetic." If your portfolio shows too many styles and techniques, it will give the art director an impression that you're an amateur who hasn't made a commitment to a particular style.

Now you might ask, why should you be penalized for having a diverse talent? Why can't art directors tell how talented you are by just looking at your work? If they like a particular style, why can't they just ask you to do a piece in that style?

These are logical and reasonable questions, but that's not how the illustration and design market works. An art director who can afford to pay for illustrations has many resources to help him locate the appropriate artist. He has his own file, gathered from research and promotional materials, and he has dozens of design annuals, illustration directories, and trade magazines to look through. When he hires an artist, he is hiring him for what he does best. He is hiring the best artist he can afford for a particular style.

So don't stock your portfolio like a big department store, offering everything from abstract paintings to watercolor realism, even though you may be quite competent in all these areas. Instead, think boutique, so art directors come to you because you have something unique to offer. People go to The Gap for basic jeans and cotton shirts, and they go to Brooks Brothers for suits. To establish your reputation, you too must offer a specialized style and technique.

An art director needs to see a collection of work in the same style so he can evaluate how you apply the style to different concepts and how he can apply your illustrations to his project. So choose a style you want to market, then create a series of ten to twenty pieces for your portfolio. It may take you a while, but it's worth the time if it helps you make your portfolio look more creative and professional.

Many artists establish themselves in one area first, then cross over to other markets as they develop a reputation and more business contacts. They eventually prepare several different portfolios for specific markets.

For example, an illustrator may do a series of drawings geared toward the editorial market, which might include illustrations of scenes from short fiction or conceptual pieces that can be used with articles on dieting, politics, or dating. And this same illustrator may develop another portfolio geared toward the advertising market, with drawings of brand name products. The style for all the drawings may be the same, but showing different subject matters will help demonstrate how your work is appropriate to your client's special area.

You can adapt your signature style to different categories by emphasizing certain elements in your illustrations:

- Book covers and magazine fiction call for narrative illustration that evokes a mood or ambience.
- Magazine articles need conceptual, intellectual, or abstract treatments.
- Advertising demands more realistic illustrations, with tighter lines and forms.
- Promotional brochures use illustrations that are more decorative in style.

Another solution is to file your illustrations under different subjects, and select the appropriate pieces for individual art directors, such as birds and flowers for an art director of a gardening magazine; gloves and jewelry for an art director of a department store.

Here are some possible categories:

- Magazines: narrative scenes/political commentaries/lifestyles/portraits/food
- Department stores: fashion/homeware/eyewear

- Advertising: cars/household products/food
- Corporate public relations: portraits/buildings/business machines/furniture
- Record companies: celebrity portraits/abstract images/poetic images

## DESIGN PORTFOLIOS

A graphic design portfolio should show a variety of projects that demonstrate your capability for solving all types of design problems. It may include corporate logos, stationery sets, packaging, brochures, posters, etc. Although the projects in your portfolio may vary in graphic solutions and style, the level of taste and craft must remain consistent.

If you're meeting a client that you know is looking for sophisticated design, show only beautiful, sophisticated projects. Don't throw in a couple of logos that you've recently designed for a discount store. It'll just confuse the client and weaken your image as an upscale designer.

Though most designers eventually do a variety of design projects, you may want to gear your portfolio toward related areas, since it's difficult to master them all in the early stages of your career. Clients are reluctant to hire designers who don't have samples that relate directly to their special needs.

## PORTFOLIO PITFALLS

What makes a weak design portfolio? Employers often cite the following three points as major stumbling blocks to getting hired:

*1. Boring images and concepts.* Images are not fresh, not striking enough to grab the viewer's attention. Concepts are not very original, not clever or witty enough to entertain. When graphic solutions are not clearly thought out, they give the reviewer the impression that you're not very innovative and therefore not a good problem solver.

*2. Lack of sensitivity to type.* This includes not paying enough attention to type spacing; matching inappropriate type to various images or projects; or not effectively integrating type with design.

*3. Absence of craft.* A sloppy presentation is an indication that you either don't have good mechani-

cal skills or that you're too lazy to pay attention to details.

If you find any of these problems in any of your pieces, weed them out and redesign them. Never remind potential employers that you're capable of producing mediocre work.

## ORGANIZING YOUR PORTFOLIO

In most cases, an art director only has about ten minutes to review your book, so choose images that will make the greatest impact. Start with a breathtaking image and end with a memorable one. The average number of pieces can range anywhere from ten to twenty.

Your presentation format will depend on the type of project you're showing and how much money you're willing to spend on transparencies, laminations, and printing.

Tearsheets (printed pieces that feature your design or artwork) are great to show because they demonstrate that you have professional experience. They're even more impressive if your clients consist of well-known art directors and major corporations. The fact that these people could hire anybody in the world and they hired you will make young art directors or marketing directors feel more comfortable about hiring you. They can justify their decision to their bosses by pointing out that you've worked for IBM or Coca-Cola.

However, if you no longer feel these tearsheets represent your style, or that the work simply doesn't live up to your current standards, then don't include them. If your current work is much better, then these tearsheets will only look out of place. Many designers and illustrators have started over by showing only newly created unpublished pieces. Good work will sell even without an IBM endorsement. Be sure to protect your best tearsheets by having them laminated or preserved in vinyl sleeves.

A popular format for many professional illustrators is to show a series of $8 \times 10$ transparencies. Your original works may come in several different sizes, and may not lend themselves to neat presentation. In that case, they should be photographed and reproduced as transparencies. When produced by a large format camera, 8 × 10 transparencies faithfully capture the original artwork. Transparencies presented in a box-like portfolio case give you a neat, accessible presentation. All the art director has to do is put them on a light box or hold them up against a window.

Originals are certainly acceptable if they are presented neatly. Make sure that corners are not torn and the surfaces are not dusty and scratched. You can leave them in protective vinyl sleeves or have each one matted with black, gray, or white matte board (using neutral-colored matte boards won't detract from your artwork).

Using originals is the least expensive way to put together a portfolio, but it does have drawbacks. In a drop-off situation, you could lose sleep over irreplaceable pieces being lost or stolen.

Use slides only if you can be there to operate the projector. Bring your own slide projector or check with the art director to make sure one is available. I don't recommend leaving slides in a drop-off situation. Many art directors will find them too troublesome.

Slides can also be used to supplement your regular portfolio. After you show a series of originals or transparencies in large format, you may want to show newly produced images in several pages of slides. The art director can view them on her light table.

## WHAT DO YOU SAY?

If you're dealing with clients who have an art background, very few words are necessary during a portfolio review session. Art directors know what they're looking for, and they know good work when they see it. For pieces that need some explaining, you may want to tell the reviewer about the client, your concept for the image, and the feeling you're trying to convey.

Don't ever say, "My work looks like so and so's." Imitating somebody else's style is still taboo in this business. It's okay for the art director to say, "I'm looking for that poetic Brad Holland feel," but it's not okay for you to somehow imply that you can imitate Brad Holland.

For graphic design, when you're dealing with a client with an art background, once again, don't

oversell. Just explain your concept for each project and allow the art director to draw her own conclusion. However, for clients from a business background, you may want to point out the strength of your style by mentioning that it's elegant, or that it's witty and humorous. Explain how your visual concept solves the client's marketing problems. The golden rule is, don't sound like a vacuum cleaner salesman; nobody is going to pay five hundred dollars for a drawing just because you're in love with your own work.

## PACKAGING YOUR WORK...AND YOURSELF

The graphic arts field is an image-conscious business, and how you present yourself and your work is important. Don't stick your work in a beat-up portfolio case and hope the art directors will recognize you as an artistic genius the minute they see your work. (Remember, most artistic geniuses are discovered after their demise!) Pay attention to every detail of your presentation, down to the portfolio that encases your artwork. It doesn't mean you have to spend five hundred dollars on an imported alligator bag, but it helps to choose something that's durable, tasteful, accessible, and easy to maintain. Your portfolio is going to travel many miles. There'll be times when you'll have to leave it with strangers for several days or hand it over to the post office, so buy something that can adequately protect your masterpieces.

## BUYING TIPS

All portfolios basically look alike, don't they? They're all black, and they all have handles, and they all have big zippers. So why are there price differences? I consulted with a portfolio buyer at a major art supply store in New York, and he gave me some buying tips.

He contends that the best portfolio cases are made in Europe, particularly in France. And he insists that man-made materials like heavy cordura mounted on heavy polypropylene or heavy vinyl, are much more durable than leather. "Most people buy leather for the looks, not for durability," he points out. Expensive cases usually come with a "multi-o-ring" mechanism, while cheaper cases come with a three-ring binder. The multi-o-ring gives the vinyl sleeves a better grip and it looks more elegant because the ring size is generally smaller. Portfolio handles that are attached by rivets are more durable than retractable handles. Most expensive portfolios (seventy-five dollars and up) should last at least five years with normal use (limited handling by UPS).

If you're showing a set of $8 \times 10$ transparencies, then choose a portfolio made especially for photographers. They usually look like attaché cases and open 180° so clients can easily take transparencies out of the box, and drop them back in after they look through them.

In the art store you might also find portfolios that look cute and sexy. You know, the type of cases that are either made of a funky wet-look pink vinyl or molded out of icy blue lucite. Of course you can use these, too; it's a free country. But they are intended for fashion models, and they may not adequately protect your artwork.

## DRESS FOR SUCCESS

Don't you just hate a book that tells you how to dress? Well, I don't blame you. After all, what do clothes and fancy portfolio cases have to do with your talent and your work? The truth is, they have absolutely nothing to do with your work, but they do have something to do with your career advancement.

After years of observation, I have concluded that there is something to the saying, "Dress for success," even for artists. Let's look at things from your client's perspective: He is meeting you for the first time, he likes your work, but your hair is a mess, your jeans are covered with paint and ketchup stains, and your shoes look like they've been through World War III.

He doesn't know that just last Tuesday, you saved a little girl's life by fighting off a vicious bulldog or that only last month you broke a date with the man of your dreams just so you could complete an assignment two days ahead of schedule for an insecure young art director. Your client has no knowledge of your admirable past.

He only knows that he has an important project that's costly to produce, difficult to execute, and it must be done on time or his boss is going to have a frightful fit.

He looks at you, and he can't tell whether you look the way you do because you're a creative genius who devotes your whole existence to creating great works of art or that you're simply on drugs. Can he trust you with a thirty thousand dollar project? Are you going to freak out and skip town when the pressure gets to be too much? Do you see all the things that go through a client's mind when he is making hiring decisions?

My advice is to save your rebellious energy for crucial moments when you have to fight for the integrity of your work, and always remember to dress respectfully for client meetings.

So what should you wear? A three-piece suit? A two thousand dollar Chanel ensemble? Let's not get too carried away. You don't want to look like a printing salesman; that would really turn off the hip, avant garde art directors. You want to project an image of success (you can demand more money this way), not an image of a struggling artist who's willing to work for peanuts. You want to look like you get enough work to pay the rent and still have money left over to buy nice clothes. You want your clothes to say: "Yes! I'm organized, I'm a 'together' person. I can handle the job!"

# Competitive Portfolios

## AN OUTSTANDING STUDENT PORTFOLIO

John Norman was recruited by Richards Brock Miller Mitchell & Associates (RBMM&A), a top design firm in Dallas, immediately after he graduated from East Texas State University. "When we look at a portfolio, we want to see work that we wish we had done ourselves," says Dick Mitchell, one of the principals at RBMM&A. "The work in the book must look professional enough to be presented to our clients. John's book shows he has tremendous potential as a designer."

Norman's portfolio was developed over a period of three years while he was a graphic design major at East Texas State University. Most of the pieces in his portfolio were class assignments. Norman's comprehensive portfolio of seventeen pieces covers all the bases. It shows he has great concepts, impeccable technical skills, enthusiasm for design, a sense of humor, and exceptional problem-solving abilities. The portfolio demonstrates his tremendous potential as a designer. We'll take a look at six projects from his portfolio.

© John Norman. Used with permission.

This assignment was to create packaging for a pasta product. Norman devised a playful box where the wavy noodles can be integrated into the design as the man's shirt ruffles. This project demonstrates that he has a flair for three-dimensional design.

This is a promotional poster for Character Typehouse. The concept was to create a seek-and-find word puzzle with forty different typefaces. Norman found the typefaces in an old type book, cut out each letter by hand, pasted them up on a piece of white board, and then shot a stat. Next, he handcolored some of the typefaces. This piece shows how Norman can create a pretty design using only type treatment.

SAPPORO

舞子

Another concept for the pasta packaging assignment. This one takes on an oriental flavor, where the noodles are encased in a bamboo box. Norman made the bamboo case with plaster, and then hand painted it.

Here Norman created a poster for the Pyramid Room, one of the most romantic restaurants in Dallas. Look closely, and you'll see a wine glass, a pair of eyes, and two faces looking at each other. Norman created this delicate illustration using airbrushing techniques. He also hand lettered the type.

This is a cheerful logo for a store called the Toy Box. Notice how the little graphic toy shapes spell out the shop's name.

THE      DALLAS      FRIDAY

KOOL      TEXAS      MAY 5, 1986

JAZZ      REUNION      8:00 P.M.

This is the last piece in Norman's portfolio. It's a poster for the Kool Jazz Festival. "This piece shows that I can work with a photographer," he explains. Norman came up with the visual concept, made a comp, and went to the photography department in search of a promising photographer to help him execute the visual concept. He found a photographer and together they spent an entire night on the shoot. Norman ended his portfolio with this memorable image.

## A Young Professional's Portfolio

When Thomas Guarneri graduated from Parsons School of Design in 1987, he had a variety of projects in his student portfolio, including posters, stationery sets, packaging, brochures, and editorial design. It was his editorial pieces that landed him a job as associate art director at *Print*, a magazine for the graphic arts industry. At *Print*, Guarneri was given an opportunity to design many projects, including magazine pages, books, award certificates, and stationery sets for special events. Within two years, Guarneri was able to revamp his portfolio with many full-color published pieces to establish himself as an upscale designer.

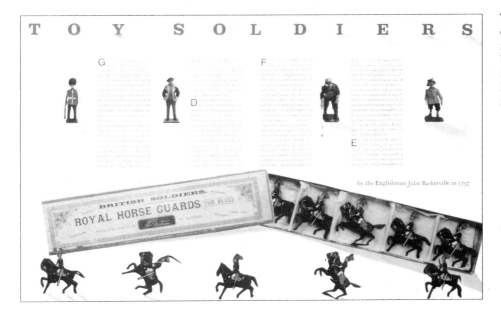

These magazine layouts were created for a student assignment. Notice how the type is beautifully integrated with images. These pages helped land him a job at *Print* magazine.

At *Print*, Guarneri was able to do the kind of work that established him as an upscale designer. He created these handsome type designs for *The Print Regional*, which showcases the winning graphics from *Print's* annual graphic design and illustration competition.

If a phrase can describe the current design climate in the Southwest, it would have to be pragmatic optimism. The first half of the year found many designers there experiencing an upswing in business. They speak enthusiastically of turnarounds and diversification—projects for clients in a growing range of industries beyond oil, real estate and finance. Yet they also speak realistically, pointing out that while the prognosis is good, economic recovery has been slow. Following the national pattern, advertising agencies have merged and design firms have expanded their services. This strengthening of resources should ultimately benefit designers as the Southwest's economy continues to evolve.

In Dallas, a new symphony hall is nearing completion, Southland Corporation has inaugurated its vast Cityplace complex, and there is talk of building a second major airport. Houston now boasts a $90-million performing arts center. The city's real estate is attracting foreign investment, a local firm has contracted to market the Soviet Union's space data and hardware, and the Port of Houston has regained its lead in foreign trade. San Antonio is leading the leisure-market front: Sea World has opened a theme park there and the city is actively seeking professional sports franchises, having passed a referendum to build a 65,000-seat dome stadium. For Texas's westernmost towns, like El Paso, light industry is blossoming along the Mexican border. Albuquerque, New Mexico, will spend the next four years building a performing arts center and raising its skyline with a 22-story office-retail complex. And the Mexican-village style Mercado retail center will revitalize Phoenix, Arizona's downtown district, as will a planned sports arena.

All this activity—and the income it will generate—should make the 1990s a big decade for the Southwest. Meanwhile, the region's designers are already seeing improvements. Sibley/Peteet Design in Dallas, as well as Steven Sessions, Hanagriff King Design, and Gluth, Weaver Design, all of Houston, report that business has picked up.

SHR Design Communications of Scottsdale, Arizona, whose local business has increased some 20 per-cent, is directly involved in helping the region attract fresh investment. The firm, whose client base is primarily national, has produced an ad campaign for a group of Phoenix businesses that dispels the bad

press about the city's economy along with some myths (it's not a waterless desert) while it positions Phoenix as the hub of the Southwest. Richardson or Richardson is doing its part to carve an image for Phoenix as a major design center with "On the Edge," an international conference held at the rim of the Grand Canyon. The conference, co-sponsored with the Phoenix Society of Communicating Arts and slated to be a biannual event, may also combat what Valerie Richardson sees as the regular exodus of the city's best talents to New York and Los Angeles.

In Austin, Texas, the reverse is true, with design activity on the rise. "There's a lot of talent concentrated here and the best people have hung on," says Tom Curry, who runs Prickly Pear Studio. Submissions to the Regional Annual this year were outstanding enough to grant Austin a section of its own for the first time.

Many southwestern designers, illustrators and photographers have stayed put and developed national reputations with the help of advances in communications technology. Conference calls, facsimile machines and overnight couriers have, they claim, virtually broken their isolation to link them with the business and design worlds. "Clients are looking for creative people, it doesn't matter where they're from," says Rick Vaughn of Vaughn/Wedeen in Albuquerque.

A national client base has enabled Sullivan Perkins of Dallas to survive tough times. What's missing, Mark Perkins points out, is "the gravy," the local projects that once walked in the door. Bringing them back or s[...]
Sloan of San Antonio voi[...]
feel when she describes [...]
felt before" that elimina[...]
experimental work. Ye[...]
recession has been heal[...]
ers to be creative and i[...]
better work on smaller [...]

That fact, plus man[...]
expansion, has literally [...]
sign. The native whim[...]
given way to somber ind[...]
edge—eccentric design[...]
—*Valerie Francene Bro[...]*

The design markets that make up what we call the South are far from homogeneous, yet designers from the majority of them report similar challenges in the past year—expanding business, better talent, increased competition, and the need to look beyond local and even regional markets for support. All of these challenges are not unrelated.

As a major component of the Sun Belt, the South is one of the fastest-growing sections of the country. Designers in some markets, particularly those along the Eastern Seaboard and in Florida, reported a generally expanding population—and economy. For them, the past year saw more work and larger profits, even if budgets remained stable or increased only slightly over the modest expenditures of the previous years.

Some of that new population has included designers, illustrators and other creative types relocating from other parts of the country, or shifting within the South itself. In addition, recent graduates of southern design schools are more often opting to remain in the South. These new talents, say several sources, are changing the creative end of the business. Too, a growing design awareness as a result of a pervasive design press works to heighten creativity. Says David Stantzen in Atlanta, "What I see emerging is a lot of young people who are committed to doing good work. With the ever-increasing sophistication of design out there, more clients are demanding it." "The quality of work here is rising dramatically," adds Don Harbor in Norfolk, Virginia. "A lot of people who were doing mediocre work a few years ago are today doing work that would stand up in any part of the country."

The rise in quality has enabled both advertising agencies and designers to become strong contenders for national accounts. Joe Ivey reports that all of the accounts at his agency in Raleigh, North Carolina, are with national advertisers except one—a regional bank. In fact, he claims, "It's fairly typical now for agencies in this area to be competing with other national agencies."

Still, if agencies in the region are taking a national focus, their number one complaint is that too many of the region's top assignments go elsewhere—i.e., to shops in Chicago, Los

Angeles, or New York. Graphic designers, too, voice the same complaint. "There are creative and talented people here," says Tom Russell of Whittle Communications in Knoxville, Tennessee, "but major corporations are doing major things in major ways in other places. If they need a logo designed, it's not done here." "Too much work, specifically some of the larger jobs and accounts, go out of town, and for what I consider no valid reason," says Murray Gaby from his agency in Miami. "The talent is here."

This underlying belief in the talent of the region, coupled with a prevailing optimism about the marketplace, characterized most of our discussions with designers in the South. At the same time, many were looking for ways to sharpen their own competitive edge. For smaller design firms and one-person studios, this can mean installing sophisticated CAD systems that cut down design time and production costs. In one large agency, computers have underscored the business end of advertising, as technology clearly displays which people and accounts are most profitable—and which are not.

But if pressures are mounting, designers and art directors in the South are finding that working for one another, as a community, is easing some of the strain. With recently formed or impending chapters in Raleigh (North Carolina), Jacksonville (Florida), Birmingham (Alabama), Atlanta (Georgia), Knoxville (Tennessee), and South Florida, the American Institute of Graphic Arts (AIGA) is receiving applause all around, both for raising design consciousness and for bringing far-flung designers into the mainstream. "Having the AIGA here has made people more aware," says Russell, "not just to be in the AIGA, but to work cooperatively and to exchange ideas, to bring the community together as one." "There's a healthier competition here now," says Meg Revelle in Raleigh, North Carolina. "One of the missions of the AIGA here is to educate people as to why design is good for business and the environment. It's a slow process, but once you raise that level of expectation, people are willing to buy better design, to search out the competition to find the best mesh. Designers here no longer have to align themselves with an ad agency to be seen as credible."—*Rose DeNeve*

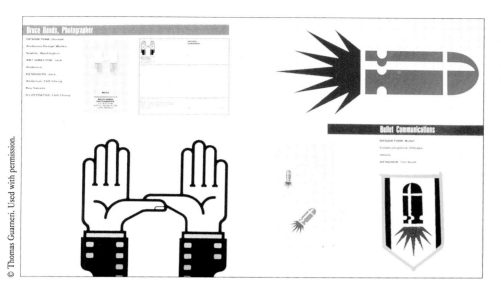

© Thomas Guarneri. Used with permission.

Pages from the book, *Print's Best Logo Design*, published by *Print* and F&W Publications. Guarneri designed the book cover and the interior pages.

Fancy stationery for *Print's* graphic competition.

## An Illustrator's Portfolio

Masuda, an illustrator based in New York City, started out as a graphic designer, but when she developed a portfolio for her painterly illustrations and a series of chic black-and-white illustrative logos, her career really took off. Her work was published in consumer magazines, and Bloomingdale's has given her regular print ad assignments. Now she has a portfolio for graphic design and a portfolio for illustration. These pieces are from her illustration portfolio. They show how she adapted her special style and technique to a variety of subjects.

Her portfolio starts with this powerful personal piece. A fashionable young woman with a portfolio enters a world of uncertain future.

© 1990 Coco Masuda

This promotional piece for the
trendy fashion store, Fiorucci,
displays her tasteful design
style.

This piece was commissioned
by *Working Woman* for an article
entitled "The DOS Mess."
Here she demonstrates how her
style can work for high-tech
subjects.

COCO MASUDA

Illustration & Design In Style

1 UNION SQUARE WEST, SUITE 803
NEW YORK NY 10003
Tel: 212.255.7381
Fax: 212.727.0694

These chic black-and-white illustrative logos opened doors for Masuda at the trendy New York City department store, Bloomingdale's.

# Persuasive Presentations

As a designer, you'll find that your client is often a committee of several people, which may consist of two vice presidents, a marketing director and a public relations manager. After your print portfolio has been reviewed by one of the committee members, you may be invited back to give a formal presentation to everyone. In a big meeting environment, a slide presentation is the most effective marketing tool.

## Show Time

When the lights go dim and the room grows silent, you're on stage! Your captive audience expects you to put on a good show. A good slide presentation must be interesting enough to stop your potential clients from dozing off in the dark. The images on the screen must be sharp and vibrant, and the project you show must have some relevance to your client's needs.

There is nothing more irritating than having to view thirty badly photographed slides. So, please, no "homemade" slides. All slides should be photographed by a professional photographer or a professional lab. If you want to keep costs down, try trading in your design services. Call a pro and offer to do his next promotional brochure if he'll shoot slides of your design pieces. Be at the shoot and make sure the lighting and styling are consistent from one slide to the next. Don't use distracting multi-colored background materials or props. They'll make the images look cluttered.

### What to show

In a slide presentation people expect to see printed work, not comps, and not personal projects. That's why it's important for you to fight for great design projects early in your career, even if you have to do them pro bono. Real-life experience is what gives you the confidence to tell the stories behind the projects flashing on the screen. Choose projects that are appropriate to the company you wish to approach. After all, a lamp manufacturer has no need for a restaurant menu, and a restaurant has no need for informational guides.

### Organization

First, choose the projects you want to show to your potential client. Then separate the slides into different categories, such as packaging, posters, brochures, corporate identity programs, and informational guides. Or you can divide the images into the different companies you've worked for, such as AT&T, Trump's Taj Mahal, Holiday Inn, and Springfield Mall.

You can show the slides in this order:

- *Slide 1:* Your company logo
- *Slide 2:* Title for the first series of images, such as "packaging" or "AT&T"
- *Slides 3 through 9:* Various packaging designs, or projects you've done for AT&T
- *Slide 10:* Title slide for the second series of images, such as "Posters" or "Trump Casino"

Repeat the pattern until all the categories are covered, and end the show with an image of your company logo. Unless your office looks like it belongs on the pages of *Architectural Digest*, skip office snapshots. Who wants to see boring pictures of an ordinary office anyway? Try to keep the show under twenty-five minutes, so your audience won't get bored, and there will be time left for questions and answers.

As you show these slides, you should be informing your viewers about the background of each project. Who's the client? What kind of businesses are they in? What are their marketing problems? Why are your concepts and design treatments appropriate to the projects? Try to be brief and to the point; don't linger too long on any one image, because you want to make the whole viewing as interesting and as entertaining as possible.

At some point, you may want to mention some of the interesting printing techniques you've used for special projects, or how you saved one client on the cost of color separations by using three colors. On some projects, you may want to show "before" and "after" slides. When you show an old logo and a new and improved logo side by side, the value of your design service will be instantaneously apparent to your viewers. With a smart visual demonstration you can help educate your client on the value of good design without lecturing on good taste and thereby sounding like a militant design freak.

When you're panning the old design, don't go overboard. It'll make you sound mean spirited. Just point out the new improvements, and how the new logo is sharper, cleaner, bolder, and more up to date.

Redesigning a logo is a sensitive issue. One of your potential clients may express concerns about tampering with a company logo that's been in place since 1957. Here, you may want to reassure him that many major corporations have done a trademark redesign in the last ten years, among them Dole, Black & Decker, the New York Stock Exchange, and the Sun Company. Point out that a redesign doesn't have to be dramatic; it can be just a '90s version of a logo that's thirty years out of date.

Another difficult question that may be thrown at you is your fee for various projects. You're not obligated to disclose these figures. However, you can give clients a ballpark figure of how much you might charge for similar projects today just to give them an idea of your price range.

Some clients distrust what they see on the screen. Always bring some printed samples with you, so viewers can examine your work closely. Also, prepare a leave-behind package for every member on the committee. This package should include samples of your work, a list of your clients, your résumé, press clippings (if you have any), and a business card.

### Illustrators' options

For illustrators, a slide presentation is less of a marketing tool and more of a promotional device, because most clients are designers or art directors. When you're dealing with one person, there is no need for such a big production. However, it is a good idea to keep a set of your best slides handy. You may be invited to give lectures at your local art directors club or at local colleges on a moment's notice.

## PRESENTING YOUR DESIGN

After you get an assignment, your job as a salesperson is still not over. It takes a great presentation to convince a demanding or insecure client to approve the design you've created for his product. To make the approval process less painful, you must develop a presentation that earns your client's trust and respect, so they'll see you as an expert in the field of visual communication, and not just as an artist with a pair of talented hands.

To accomplish this, you have to prepare your presentation like Perry Mason prepares for a court case. You must defend your work by demonstrating the logic behind your concept and color selections. You want the client to believe that your design is effective, both from a marketing and an aesthetic standpoint.

Keep in mind that, as a professional designer, you have many years of art training. Intuitively, you know what constitutes good design. Your clients usually do not have an art background, and therefore may not be on the same wavelength as you in terms of taste. So if you can't defend your work from a business standpoint, you may end up having to make a lot of changes, just because your client can't see that it's a big deal to change a black-and-blue logo into a green-and-yellow one. Major design changes are not only time consuming, but the changes requested by your client may seriously compromise the integrity of your original artistic vision. The sad result is that you'll be doing work you don't believe in, and the client will end up buying a piece of bad art that won't help him move the product.

To come up with persuasive sales pitches for your design, you can't create the work in a vacuum. You must learn about the product and its market. For example, if you are designing a bottle label for a natural soft drink, you have to consider the type of consumer who is willing to spend $1.25 for a bottle of soda, when a Coke only costs 75 cents. You have to get to know the product's competitors. What are the weaknesses and strengths of their labels? How can you design a label that will allow the new product to stand out in a sea of natural soft drinks? Once you've identified the marketing problem, you can then come up with a design solution that can be intelligently explained at the presentation meeting.

One way to impress your client is to present many different concepts and design variations. It shows that you've worked hard for the assignment and that you could come up with more than one graphic solution. Clients like choices. But keep in mind that, although quantity is impressive, quality control is more important. Part of your job as a designer is to help the client choose the best design for his product. If you give him twelve design options and only eight truly have merit, you risk having the client choose a bad design. So if you don't want to take a chance on doing something you're not going to be proud of, edit your work carefully before showing it to the client.

Always present your ideas in a professional manner. Crumpled tissue paper makes even great ideas look uninspired. So present all of your sketches on black, white, or gray matte boards. Find out at what stages your client would like to review the work—at the early conceptual phase, when you can show rough sketches or marker comps, or at a more completed stage, when you can show a comp that is very close to the finished product.

If you suspect that your client may have problems visualizing roughs or marker comps, then create comps that are as close to the finished product as possible. Chances are, clients are less likely to request major changes when they see a realistic comp. However, high-quality comps can be expensive and time consuming to produce, so always work a realistic comp cost into your budget estimate.

If you can anticipate your clients' business concerns, it will help you explain your work in a language they can understand and appreciate. Read your clients' business magazines to get a better understanding of their perspectives. Publications like *Business Week*, *Forbes*, *Adweek's Marketing Week* and *Marketing and Media Decisions* can help you learn more about marketing strategies. When your client comes to believe that you are creating a design with the company's best interests at heart, then they'll trust your design judgment. And you can concentrate on producing great design instead of worrying about compromises.

## ILLUSTRATORS' PRESENTATIONS
As an illustrator, presenting your work is much less complicated. For one thing, illustrators usually work inside a well-defined context, either for a magazine article, an annual report, or a book cover. Your clients are often art directors or designers, visual people who know what they're looking for. When an illustrator gets an assignment, he discusses possible concepts for the project with the art director and goes home to work on the piece. He can present a dozen possible concepts to the art director with rough thumbnail sketches or two or three concepts on 8 × 10 drawing paper. It's basically a two-step process: The art director approves one particular sketch and the illustrator goes home and executes it. He doesn't face the same type of conceptual presentation that designers must face, because the main concept for the project is worked out at the design stage.

# Developing Persuasive Presentations

To show you how a small advertising agency develops and makes presentations, we enlisted the help of Martha Voutas Productions, Inc. Martha Voutas started her firm in 1978 as a one-woman design firm. Today, it is a full-service design firm/advertising agency with a staff of five. The firm now bills over one and a half million dollars annually and boasts an impressive fashion client list, including Perry Ellis, Liz Claiborne, Izod Lacoste, Optica Eyewear, Chaus, and Kinney Shoe Corporation.

"My first major client was Perry Ellis, and with Perry you couldn't show him sketches or rough comps. You had to show him exactly what the final design would look like. I've since found that most of my clients are that way. They want to see exactly what they're getting, especially if the project is three-dimensional, like packaging or display units," says Voutas.

## PRESENTATION I — ELECTION CAMPAIGN LOGOS

Several months before the 1988 presidential election, many design firms were invited to submit design ideas for the Dukakis/Bensten campaign logo. Thirty design firms from across the country submitted visual concepts. After viewing all thirty designs, Michael Dukakis selected the comp submitted by Martha Voutas Productions.

Like most election graphics, the image was simple and straightforward. It was a waving American flag with the candidate's name printed over it. The unique thing about this flag was that the edges on the stars and stripes had a rough finish, giving it a hand-drawn effect, and it projected a warmer, friendlier feeling for this traditionally patriotic image.

Though Dukakis/Bensten lost the election in November, Voutas says she's happy that her firm played a part in America's political history. "It's wonderful to see thousands of people waving your design across the TV screen," she says.

For the formal presentation, MVP made up realistic comps of the promotional signs with hand-cut PMS (Pantone Matching System) paper. The type was made with 3M color keys and was printed on an acetate overlay.

© Martha M. Voutas. Used with permission.

The smaller image was designed for car stickers, while the large signs were for store windows and for Dukakis supporters to wave at a campaign rally.

Designs for the buttons were presented on fabrics to show how the graphic stands out on garments.

Almost no design changes were requested. The final printed products, with the exception of minor type changes to accommodate both of the candidates' names, looked just like the comps.

## PRESENTATION II – HANGTAGS AND SHOPPING BAGS

The Liz Claiborne Corporation was opening several new stores named First Issue. MVP was working for Claiborne on retainer. Voutas came up with the idea to play up the store's name, by using stamp graphics for the store's promotional items, such as shopping bags and hangtags for the clothes.

"We bought an antique book on stamp collecting in a stamp collector's store and we used it for reference. By coincidence, an assistant to a Claiborne vice president had a stamp collection from his grandfather, and he brought in all his grandfather's stamps. Together with the client, we selected stamps that would be appropriate for this project."

The stamps chosen had an elegant, old-world feel. All of them involved intriguing drawings. Different images were chosen for different lines of clothes. For example, the image of a buffalo was used for the jeanswear group.

The stamps were made into large stats. MVP designers then reworked the stamp by eliminating unnecessary information on the artwork. "We removed the typography and cleaned up some of the complex lines in the drawing. We were able to do this because these were copyright-free stamps."

In addition to revising the existing stamps, the firm also made a stamp with artwork from clip art and hired freelance illustrators to create an additional three different stamp designs.

Once the stamps were completely revised and designed, they were sent out for INT (Imaging and Transfer) colors, which are colors used for dry transfer. "We had the artwork reduced to actual stamp size, then printed on white paper, and we cut them out to look like real stamps," explains Voutas.

At the presentation meeting, everything was shown to actual scale, from hangtags to shopping bags. The clients approved the project with very minor changes.

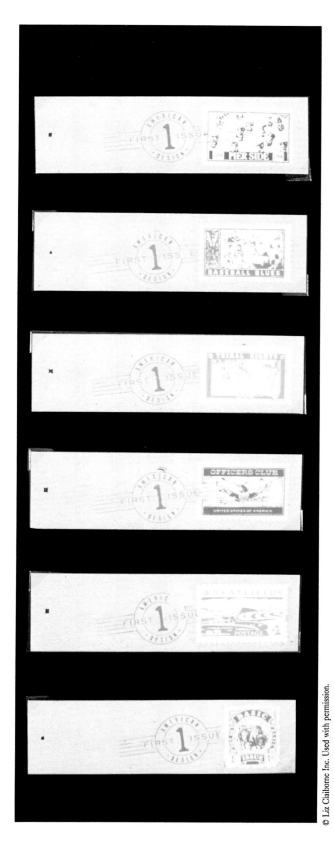

These hangtags are comps that were shown to the client. The black postal date mark was designed by Martha Voutas based on an actual First Issue cancellation.

The printed shopping bags look just like the comps. The bag with the image of the clipper ship was created with the help of clip art.

# PRESENTATION III – CLOTHES LABELS FOR ALEXANDER JULIAN

When you work with a fashion designer, even the inside label must be designed to reflect the designer's image. For Alexander Julian's line of women's wear, MVP designed these handsome labels.

First MVP created many color combination bars by pasting together pieces of colored papers that reflect the line's rich, dark classic colors.

Then the client is shown color bars with an italic type.

The final cloth labels were printed in the colors suggested by MVP, but the type is printed in roman, not italic.

# PRICING FOR PROFIT

**M**oney. It stands for power, security, and freedom. The thought of it conjures up so much emotion that most of us would rather not discuss it. Yet as a freelancer, you are forced to talk money all the time. Negotiating for the right price is part of the challenge of being a successful professional artist.

Although the Graphic Artists Guild publishes a book on current market rates (*Handbook of Pricing & Ethical Guidelines*) every year, it readily admits that there are no standard rates because each job's circumstances are different.

Prices vary due to many factors, such as how much your client is willing to pay, the complexity of the project, and the current value of your product in the marketplace. Supply and demand determines the value of your work. For the first two or three years, most artists take on any job that comes along to get exposure and valuable tearsheets for their portfolios. If you market yourself vigorously by knocking on all the right doors, within the first two years you should get a fairly good idea of how receptive the market is to your particular style of illustration.

For instance, if you get regular assignments from major advertising agencies or national consumer magazines, you may value your work at a high level, and set your minimum by prices listed in the current issue of the Graphic Artists Guild's *Pricing & Ethical Guidelines*. When a client calls, he may start negotiating by quoting figures listed in the *Guide*. Of course, when you're self-employed, you have the freedom to break your own rules, and illustrators and designers frequently do. If things are slow one month, you may agree to accept a lower paying job from a client who can't afford or isn't willing to pay more. Or if a high profile project comes in, and the pay rate is below your minimum, you may choose to accept the job for less than your minimum rate because the value of the exposure makes it worthwhile. And, of course, artists, like celebrities, often volunteer their services for charitable causes or exciting new ventures, such as a new literary magazine.

If the market is not immediately receptive to your current style, you must value your work below the market rate, and work for less demanding clients who have lower budgets. In that case, you have two choices: Continue with the old style and hope someday it will catch on, or develop a new style and hope it will be more marketable to higher level clients.

## PRICING ILLUSTRATION

In the illustration market, advertising and corporate work generally pay higher rates than editorial work. However, most illustrators enjoy editorial work because it offers more creativity and valuable exposure. If you do illustrations for annual reports, only the stockholders will see them, and stockholders don't usually buy illustrations. In advertising, illustrators are rarely given credit in the ad. In magazines, however, you are given credit for your piece and millions of readers will see your work. It's the quickest way to get exposure, if your work capture's art directors' imaginations.

Magazine work is the hardest area in which to negotiate for higher prices. Since most reputable magazines have established rates, the art directors will quote you these rates and they don't like to make exceptions, unless, of course, they feel you're the only person for the assignment. If the art director wants to hire a famous illustrator for a special cover, he may requisition a higher illustration budget for that one issue.

Generally speaking, magazine prices follow the rate of the magazine's circulation—the higher the circulation, the higher the illustration fees. *Time* and *Newsweek*, each with a circulation of several million, will pay three thousand dollars and up for a cover illustration. Next on the list are business magazines like *Forbes*, *Business Week*, and *Money*, which pay two thousand dollars and up for a cover and six hundred dollars for a spot illustration. *Esquire*, *The Atlantic Monthly*, *The New Yorker*, and *Rolling Stone* also pay high rates as well, at least two thousand dollars for a cover and several hundred dollars for spot drawings.

For advertising and corporate work, the rule is always ask for more, especially if the initial offer is below the market rate. The job of an art buyer is to get the best artist for the lowest price. Unless you are desperate for work, list the reasons why you deserve more. One way is to quote the market rate in the *Pricing Guide*. Another way is to assess the complexity of the work and the deadline pressure involved. For example, if you get a layout where you're asked to illustrate many different types of fruit and several products in great detail, you may point out this is a lot of work and you need a higher fee. Or if the art buyer gives you a short deadline on the project, you can say you need more money because you'll have to work late hours and weekends.

An art director called an illustrator with a job for five different book covers, all for the same famous author. The publisher wanted the illustrator because she had done another book cover for the same author and they liked the result. They offered her $15,000 for five wraparound covers, and a tight deadline (about a week per cover). The illustrator was very busy at the time and felt she couldn't complete the project within the time frame the publisher wanted. She asked for more money and more time. After all, she reasoned, she had received $3,000 for that first cover. Initially, they said no, but when she didn't change her mind, they called back a few days later with a new offer. They gave her $3,500 for each book cover and, instead of insisting on a wraparound, they agreed that she could just do the front covers. This change allowed her to do the work within the time frame the client had initially wanted.

The illustrator was in a position to negotiate, be-cause she knew that work was always available for her. She has found that when a client truly wants you, and your demands are reasonable and fair, they'll try to find ways to accommodate your request.

She says that if you never negotiate, you may get a reputation in the business as a "pushover" artist, and art buyers will always call you for low budget jobs.

When you price a job, you should take these factors into consideration:

- *Geographic scope.* Is the magazine or advertising campaign local, regional, or national? A national campaign will have a bigger budget than a local one.
- *Size of the client.* Is it a small company or a major corporation? Does the magazine have a large or small circulation?
- *Client's location.* Usually the more populated the city, the higher the rate.
- *Normal deadline or rush deadline.* If they want it that bad and that fast, they can pay you more for pushing aside other assignments.
- *Complexity of the illustration.* Generally speaking, highly detailed illustration commands a higher rate than a looser style, because more work and time is involved in completing the project.
- *Rights purchased.* Are you selling first rights or all rights?
- *The value of your style.* Is your style unique and particularly hot at the moment?
- *Your artistic reputation.* Art directors like to work with "stars," because it helps elevate their own status.
- *Unusual expenses.* Some illustrators use special materials and tools to create special effects, such as those produced with a color photocopy machine. Experimenting with a laser copier at your local copy shop can run you $50 to $150 per project. You may want to explain these special circumstances to your client and convince him to pay for the laser copying expenses.

## PRICING DESIGN PROJECTS

Negotiating prices for design projects is a much more complex task. In most cases, your potential clients will ask you to come up with an estimate without giving you a clue as to their design budget. And you will have to work out an elaborate estimate before being offered a job.

To do an estimate and proposal, you need to find out as many details as you can about the project, such as:

• What is the project for?
• How will it be used?
• How many pages?
• Color or black and white?
• How much copy needs to be set?
• Do you need to hire a photographer or illustrator?

For low-budget projects, say anything under five thousand dollars, you may want to send a letter stating that for you to design and produce camera-ready mechanicals and to supervise printing production and delivery of this project, you want a certain amount of money. Estimate how much you charge for design services, such as developing concepts, paste-up, and press checking. Then in a separate column estimate outside services such as typesetting, photography, printing, messenger services, and any other outside services.

For major projects, however, include an elaborate proposal with your estimate. To get the price you want to charge, you need to break the project down into different phases and explain your plan of operation, so your clients know how you intend to spend the money.

Start by writing a cover letter thanking the client for considering you for the job. Tell them your work philosophy, that you're excited about the project, and that you will be happy to clarify any part of the proposal the client doesn't understand. Supply your client with a copy of your résumé and a list of names of your past and present clients (put the most prestigious on top).

A proposal tells the client how you plan to execute this major design project. Here is a simple example; you can follow the general guidelines and make yours as elaborate or concise as you see fit.

## PROPOSAL FOR CORPORATE IDENTITY PROGRAM REDESIGN

### Phase I: Research

1. Consult the client on corporate history, past designs, and the image the client desires to project today.
2. Review competitors' identity programs and analyze what you can learn from their strengths and weaknesses.
3. Review client's budget and determine production limitations and possibilities.

### Phase II: Concept and Design

1. Develop several concepts based on research results.
2. Present concepts to client.
3. Review color and type selections with client.
4. Make necessary design changes and adjustments in accordance with client instructions.
5. Client approves final changes.

### Phase III: Production and Printing Supervision

1. Supervise mechanical artists on preparation of camera-ready artwork.
2. Get bids from printers.
3. Have client review layout.
4. Make final client alterations.
5. Have client review bids from printer.
6. Supervise printing to ensure color quality.
7. Delivery of final printed product to client.

Always include a cost estimate with your proposal so the client has an idea of your costs and prices for different stages of the project. See an example on the next page.

On the back of your estimate form, state the terms of your payment. Here are the major points you'll want to specify:

• Payment schedule: A typical request is one-third up front, one-third after concept approval, and one-third immediately after the completion of the final mechanicals.

- When and how you charge for revisions and customer alterations.
- State that you expect to get paid for the time spent on a project, even if the client decides to kill the project midway.
- Charge a late fee of 1 1/2 percent a month, if the bill isn't paid in thirty days.
- State the kind of rights you are selling to the client.

## Estimate for Project X

Client:
Date:
Submitted by:

Design fees:
  Research ...........................................$00
  Concept & Design ..........................$00
  Layout & Mechanicals ......................$00
Expenses:
  Typesetting....................................$00
  Illustrations ..................................$00
  Photography...................................$00
  Film & Processing...........................$00
  Presentation materials......................$00
  Stats.............................................$00
  Props............................................$00
  Travel ...........................................$00
  15% Contingency Fee ......................$00
                              Total: _____
                  Design fees & expenses _____

Most designers add a 15 to 30 percent markup for outside services. However, you may want to have the printer and typesetter bill your client directly if these expenses are too high for you to carry. Explain to your client that he will save money by paying the vendors directly.

A complete listing of these terms can be found in the *Handbook of Pricing & Ethical Guidelines* and in *Business and Legal Forms for Graphic Designers*, by Tad Crawford. Simply adapt the copy to fit your needs. Have official estimates and invoices printed up. Printing payment terms on the back of your standardized estimate form allows your client to review the terms before signing the form.

## Calculating Profits

Some designers use a simple formula for calculating their profit margins. They multiply their salaries by three: one-third for salary, one-third for overhead, and one-third for profit. Add up the amount and divide by the hours you plan to work for the year and come up with an hourly rate. For example, if you decide your salary should be $35,000 a year, you multiply that by three, and get the total sum of $105,000 a year. Divide that by 1,800 hours (based on a 35-hour week). You get about $58 an hour.

A more accurate method is to add up all your overhead (rent, health insurance, self-promotion, utilities, outside services, office and art supplies, business taxes, and salary) and divide it by 1,800 hours. That will give you your hourly rate. Since it's unlikely that you would work a full 35 hours every single week of the year, you may want to divide by a smaller number, and charge your hourly rate based on this total.

## Bidding Wars

For a major design project, the client often asks for bids from several design firms. In their eagerness to get the job, many young designers will often underbid. Bidding too low, however, almost always works against you. If your estimate for the job is substantially lower than bids from several other companies, the client may suspect that you are not experienced enough to understand the amount of work involved, or worse, that you won't be able to give him the quality he is looking for.

Not all clients go for the lowest bid, says one successful designer. "I find that if the client feels you are the designer he wants for the job, that even if your bid is too high, he will still come to you first, and try to get you to lower the price. And you can negotiate from that point on," he advised.

How do you determine a fair price? The *Pricing & Ethical Guidelines* lists the market rates, and many designers quote these figures. But many designers also take into consideration the following factors:

- Client size. Is it a small company or a major corporation?
- The complexity of the project.
- The extent of usage.
- The current market rate for comparable work.
- The value of your style, skill, and service.
- Is it a slow month for business?
- The value of the project itself. Is it a high profile job that will give you exposure to the right people? Will it help you win awards and help build your reputation?

## WORKING ON SPEC

Working on speculation is a controversial issue in the design profession. It means a client asks one or more designers to come up with design concepts for a project, then hires the designer that comes up with the best concept. Professional organizations generally discourage design professionals from engaging in this practice. After all, plumbers, doctors, and engineers don't work on spec, why should artists? They feel clients should be able to make a sound judgment by reviewing the designers' portfolio and job proposals. Another concern is that there are unscrupulous clients who just want free ideas and have no intention of hiring a designer. Some designers point out that work on spec is actually harmful to the client since designers create graphic solutions without taking the time to carefully study the client's marketing problems.

Even with all these negative factors, there are still those who regularly work on spec. One designer explains, "If you don't have a great portfolio, doing work on spec may be the only way you can get assignments."

## COLLECTING YOUR DUE

Though most of your clients will honor their payment obligations, once in a while every designer meets up with a deadbeat who simply refuses to pay. If you have the proper contracts and paper trails (signed estimates, purchase orders, approval forms for various stages of the design process), you can take your client to court, or solicit the services of the Joint Ethics Committee, an organization made up of volunteers who are knowledgeable about this industry.

The Joint Ethics Committee is sponsored by several artists organizations, including the Graphic Artists Guild and the AIGA. The service is free, but your client must agree to participate in the process, and both you and the client must abide by the final judgment handed down by the board. Since going to court can be time consuming, some illustrators and designers come up with some imaginative self-remedies. Most of them involve embarrassing the client in the spirit of creativity and good, clean fun. One design firm in Los Angeles had official rubber stamps made for late invoices. One says "Share the Wealth," and another says "Pay or Die," complete with tongue-in-cheek skull and bones logo.

There was a young designer who couldn't get her client to pay her bill. The client had ignored several invoices, and when she called him on the phone, he told her he planned to send her a check soon. After waiting five months, she decided it was time to pay him a visit. But before she did, she made an unusual prop for the occasion.

She borrowed a baseball bat from a friend, took a pair of handles off a black portfolio and neatly taped them onto the wooden bat with black tape. She went to the client's office carrying the bat in the manner she would carry a portfolio. "I walked into his office, and when he saw what I was carrying, he laughed so hard he nearly fell off his chair," she recalls with triumph. After the art director got over his laughing fit, he promptly wrote her a check for the total amount he owed her.

The young designer's clever ploy saved her time and money since she didn't have to go through the courts. Of course, this is not a safe way to get your money, especially if you look like Arnold Schwarzenegger. You could get yourself shot walking into an office with a baseball bat, and your client could claim self-defense.

The best way to protect yourself is to take care of all the legal paperwork. If you're dealing with a new client who's not an established company, try to get a least 50 percent upfront and have the client pay you the balance on delivery.

# FINDING THE RIGHT REP

After you've been through the task of selling, negotiating, and billing, the idea of working with an agent may sound like the answer to all your problems. For a fee, an agent gets you the jobs and you can be an artist again!

Sound like an ideal situation? Unfortunately, life is never that simple. For one thing, a good rep is hard to find in this business. Most established reps, with important contacts, are extremely selective about who they'll represent. They prefer to work with illustrators who are established professionals. They'll only represent young artists if they see great marketing potential in their work. As a result, many illustrators end up signing on with the first rep who's willing to work with them, and many live to regret it.

Some people who call themselves reps know very little about the commercial art business. After all, you don't need a degree to get into the repping business. Many reps have no idea how to develop an artist's career, how to present a portfolio, or how to talk to art directors. That's why most illustrators work with half a dozen reps before they find an agent they can live with. Many artists ultimately decide that they're better off without one.

The truth is, unless you're extremely shy, sensitive, temperamental, or disorganized, there is nothing a rep can do for you that you can't do for yourself. Many successful illustrators rep themselves because they feel it's important to establish a personal relationship with their clients, and most art directors still prefer to deal with artists directly.

You may find that once you get over the fear of selling your work, it can be a lot of fun, as well as being challenging. You can learn a great deal from visiting different art directors. It's a great way to pick up helpful gossip that may lead to other projects. Also, by getting the work yourself, you'll have more control over what projects to take on and for how much. Repping yourself will also help you save money, since the standard agent fee is 25 percent, and you stand to lose $250 for every $1,000 you bill.

Of course, not every artist enjoys the wheeling and dealing aspects of the business. Many prefer to concentrate all their energy on their work rather than make cold calls or collect late fees. For these artists, there is no other choice than to work with a rep. Agents also are helpful for those who want to market their work in other cities or in foreign countries.

A rep has a lot of control over your career development. He or she calls on the client, presents your portfolio, and negotiates your fees and work schedule. Some even do billing and collecting.

How your rep deals with your clients will be a reflection on you. It's important to find someone who respects you as an artist and is supportive of your career goals. You need someone who will make the extra effort to contact the right clients, someone who is a good communicator and does great follow-through so the client will want to hire you again.

In theory, a rep should be taking orders from you. You tell the rep what type of clients you want to work for, the kind of prices you want to charge, and the rep brings you the assignments. But not every rep is going to be that sweet. After all, they're in the business to make money. Some are not going to have the patience to wait around for the right clients to come along. Some are going to think that you're an artist and live in la-la-land, and they should "help" you make some "smart" career choices, either by matching you up with clients who have steady work (but not necessarily the kind of work that you want to do), or they may turn down creative projects that they don't feel pay enough, without consulting you first.

One illustrator made it clear to his first rep that he wanted to be a fashion illustrator, but the rep showed his portfolio to clients he could easily get assignments from. The illustrator ended up drawing a lot of bunny rabbits, planes, and cars for promotional brochures. He admits that the jobs helped pay his rent, but he also lost valuable time in breaking into the fashion market. After he left his rep, he concentrated his efforts on marketing to fashion magazines and department stores, and he got the fashion assignments he wanted. He felt that his rep simply gave up after getting a few rejections from fashion clients. As a result, his career didn't take off as fast as it could have.

Another illustrator complained that his first agent wanted to review everything he did before he showed it to the art director, then pressured him to make the drawings tighter, forcing him to alter the loose, fluid lines that he felt were the essence of his style. After the illustrator left his rep, he discovered that art directors preferred his natural style, and that the rep was second-guessing the art directors.

Of course, there are artists who believe they owe their careers to their caring reps. A knowledgeable rep can be a wonderful coach, teaching a talented but inexperienced artist how to dress for presentations and how to reorganize a portfolio to make it more marketable. Also, most reps are skillful negotiators. They're not selling their own work, so they can be much more aggressive in asking for the fee they feel you deserve. Another invaluable service they perform is chasing after late payments, a task many artists find painfully awkward.

If you are searching for a rep, there are many to choose from. What type is right for you depends on how much personal attention you want. Most reps fall into three categories:

*The personal rep.* This is an agent who only represents you. Most of the time, a personal rep is a spouse, friend, or relative, someone you've trained to help you handle the business end. Using a relative as a rep is quite common in the business. By using someone you trust, you know you're being represented by someone who has your best interests at heart. The down side is the strain of working so closely together in a high-pressured business atmosphere; it can destroy a personal relationship.

*Small agencies.* Small agencies can be a one-man band or a small group of reps with an office staff. These agencies take on a stable of five to thirty artists whose styles are geared to a specific market, and their agents focus their marketing efforts only in these areas. It can be editorial, publishing, advertising, or promotional. Their reputations are built on the unique styles of their artists. The advantage of being repped by a small agency is that you will receive specialized attention. The down side is, if you're lumped together with a group of mediocre artists, it can hurt your reputation and may devalue the price of your work.

*Large agencies.* These agencies handle hundreds of artists. Large agencies are more suitable for artists who specialize in a particular area, such as technical drawings or product renderings. For example, an art buyer will call one of these agencies if he needs a competent artist to draw a realistic poodle for a dog food ad. The agency will send him several cat and dog portfolios to choose from. It's a very competitive situation. Some artists will get steady work, while others may see only one or two assignments a year.

## How a Rep Works

To give you an idea of how an agency works, I visited with veteran agent Jimm Burris. Burris has worked at Mandola and the Pushpin Group in New York City. Today, Burris manages the print division at R/ Greenberg Associates, where he represents photographers.

As an artist's rep, Burris looks for illustrators who have a personal vision, with a style that is modern and "on the edge." He doesn't take on artists who are just a pair of hands ready to do anything from puppies to coffee cans. He prefers to represent artists whose work he personally admires. "It's easier to sell work that I believe in." However, he is also realistic about the marketplace; he has turned down artists whom he likes but whose work he feels is too personal or "fine-artish" for the commercial market.

Designer/illustrator Laurie Rosenwald has agents representing her across the globe. She designed these colorful business cards that name her rep in each country. She gives the cards to clients according to the country in which they are located.

Margarethe Hubauer
Erikastrasse 99
D · 2000 Hamburg 20
Telephone 040 · 48 60 03
Fax 040 · 47 77 84

Philippe Arnaud
35, Rue de la Rochefoucauld
Paris 75009 · France
Telephone 48.78.15.41
Fax 45.26.41.03

PARIS

© Laurie Rosenwald. Used with permission.

In addition to promoting artists and getting work for them, reps also set up financial arrangements and work schedules plus collect fees. Most reps charge 25 percent of the total fee charged to the client. In return, artists must do revisions when necessary, deliver work on time, and pay for promotional expenses.

When an artist receives an assignment, the rep sends job confirmation forms to the client and illustrator so both parties are clear on what has been verbally agreed. When the work is completed and accepted by the client, the rep sends a copy of the dated invoice to the illustrator. When the rep receives payment from the client, he immediately sends the illustrator his share of the fee.

At Pushpin, Burris promoted his illustrators heavily, advertising in the *Creative Black Book* and in *American Showcase*. He periodically printed poster cards, calling sheets, and brochures to send them to potential clients. Pushpin pays 25 percent of the promotional cost, and illustrators must pay the other 75 percent. Burris admits that sometimes he had to drag a few illustrators kicking and screaming into participating in costly promotional efforts.

When agencies take on an established illustrator who comes with his own list of house clients, they usually will negotiate an agreement where the illustrator may keep a limited number of house clients. "This means I don't pitch or service these clients," says Burris. Or if the illustrator desires, he or she may pay the agency a percentage of the fee to service those accounts. After the illustrator joins the agency, new clients must be referred to the agency.

When an illustrator feels he no longer needs the agency's services, the contract may be terminated. But for the next six months, a fee is usually paid to the agency for all the assignments he gets on his own. The rationale is that most of these assignments came about as a result of the agency's promotional efforts.

## SHOPPING FOR REPS

When you're ready to look for a rep, here are a few points to consider:

• Consult with art directors who deal with reps on a regular basis. Ask them who their favorite rep is, who does great follow through, which ones are good negotiators, and who gets on their nerves by being too pushy.

• Look for agencies in publications where reps advertise themselves and their artists. The *Black Book, American Showcase, The New York Gold Book, The L.A Work Book*, and *The Art Directors Index* are among the publications where agencies advertise their artists. Go through these books and find the agents who are selling your style of illustration.

• Once you've found an agent who agrees to rep you, check his references by calling up his stable of illustrators. Ask them if they feel they have been well served by their agent.

## TERMS OF AGREEMENT

Before signing a contract with your new rep, you should discuss the following concerns. Some of these points may be negotiable. It's a buyers' market.

• What's the rep's fee? Twenty-five percent is the industry standard. Anything higher than 25 percent is very unusual, and you should ask for an explanation.

• Talk to the rep about your career goals. Where do you see yourself five years from now? What type of clients do you want to work for? Clarifying these points will help your rep to plan an effective marketing strategy for you.

• How many house clients can you keep? Are you allowed to generate your own clients without involving your rep?

• What are the rep's promotional strategies? Can you afford expensive promotional projects?

• Who bills the client and who collects the fee? If the agent collects the fee, when can you expect your share? Many artists prefer to do billing themselves. You can discuss this point with your new rep.

• How much do you want to charge for your work? An experienced rep should have some idea how much your work is worth in the marketplace.

• After the working relationship is terminated, how long do you have to continue paying your rep residual commissions? (Six months is the industry standard.)

Your rep can hurt your career by being insensitive to your needs. Unprofessional reps have been known to:

- Turn down small jobs because small fees just aren't worth the paperwork, even though the work may be very creative and may help advance your career.
- Pressure you to accept a job you don't feel comfortable doing.
- Discourage you from experimenting with new techniques and styles because they may not yet be as marketable as the old style.
- Not allow clients to speak to you directly for fear of financial dealings behind the rep's back.

Getting a rep is like getting a business partner. In order for the relationship to work, there must be mutual trust and respect. You have to believe that your rep will always act in your best interest, and your rep must have confidence that when he gets you an assignment, you will complete it in a professional manner and meet the deadline.

# ARTIST'S PROFILES

The ten successful illustrators and designers featured in this section are from diverse backgrounds. For example, Javier Romero grew up in Madrid, Ty Wilson in Kansas, Marcus Von Nispel in Frankfurt, Laurie Rosenwald in New York City, and David Diaz in Florida. They have all found success in America as graphic designers or illustrators.

Though their work differs in artistic style and temperament, they seem to share a few common traits: a belief in their artistic vision, a determination to market their work, and, of course, genuine talent.

I chose to profile them because their stories are current and inspiring. Most of them are only in their thirties, yet they have managed to build professional reputations and attract high-profile clients by creating top-quality work.

These artists were honest about their beginnings and they were generous in giving advice. After all, it wasn't very long ago that they were struggling to get established in the business. They understand what young artists go through — the painful rejections and the constant self-doubts — and hope that by sharing their experiences they can help others cope with the complexities of this competitive yet rewarding business.

# *Javier Romero*

In 1980, Javier Romero left a promising advertising career in Spain and started life over again in New York City.

"My friend in Madrid asked me, 'Why are you going to America? You're doing great here. You're only twenty-five and already you're a top art director.' But that was the problem. I was moving up so fast that it just wasn't challenging for me anymore. I was looking at great work from New York's Pushpin Studio, and I thought, 'Wow! I would love to be there and create great work.' I looked at Milton Glaser's work and I wanted to be like Milton Glaser," Romero recalls.

So Romero obtained an educational grant from his government to study graphic design at the School of Visual Arts. "In the beginning I wanted to get a college degree. I was a self-taught artist and I wanted to legitimize myself. But people kept saying I was too advanced for the foundation classes and they encouraged me to take only the classes I enjoyed. So I spent a year and a half taking a broad range of courses, from graphic design to film editing. I even took a class with Milton Glaser!"

In the beginning, life was hard. "I was living on a grant and when that was spent I had no income. I was living and working in a studio apartment on West Twenty-sixth Street. I slept on a mattress next to my drawing table. I didn't speak English, and I would get a class assignment to do a book cover, but I wouldn't know what the book was about," says Romero.

After he left the School of Visual Arts, he and a friend started a small studio called Periscope Design. They did a lot of work for startup record companies, some of which ignored their bills. "When you work for a startup company, always get some money up front," advises Romero. Because of his language problem, his friend did most of the selling, and he did most of the designing. The partnership lasted for three years.

In 1984, Romero's English was better and he decided to freelance on his own. "I sent out samples of my work and I got jobs immediately. My first assignment was from *Glamour* magazine. I did little spot illustrations for their editorial pages. It was like going backward. In Madrid I was a successful art director doing major four-color advertising campaigns, and here I was doing little black-and-white spot drawings."

Nevertheless, Romero took these assignments very seriously, and soon his spot illustrations appeared in many Condé Nast publications, including *Self* and *Mademoiselle*. "I was still experimenting with different styles and techniques. I could do realistic illustrations very well, but that didn't fulfill me artistically. I wanted to get paid for my ideas and not for the craft of painting. I was attracted to the abstract modern approach — to convey a complex idea with just a few simple lines."

Once Romero felt that he had developed a personal style, he took a series of images to show a designer at Condé Nast. "She didn't like it at all. She said it was very bad, and I shouldn't do it anymore. I was crushed. I mean, I'm very critical of my own work and I felt very strongly about this style that I had developed. I was so depressed that on my way home, I nearly cried on the subway. When I got back to my studio, I said to myself, 'Now what am I going to do?' "

What he did was call *Seventeen* magazine. The art director invited him over. She loved his work so much that she gave him his first assignment for *Seventeen*.

"You have to believe in your work. Go through

Cover illustration for *TIME* magazine. Art director, Rudolph Hoglund.

the bad times. Give yourself time to develop your own style, take the time out to find out who you are," urges Romero.

Modern, bold, colorful graphics became Romero's signature style. It has gotten him important recognition in the field and more work than he can handle. Today, Romero has four assistants working for him, and he's still so busy that he turns down at least one job a week. "I think art directors are responding to the optimistic spirit of the work. I'm optimistic about the future, I'm excited about new technology, and I think my graphics reflect this optimism. The reason why it still looks fresh after all these years is because my graphics have evolved with the times. And I'm still experimenting with this style," Romero explains.

Romero doesn't have a rep. "Eighty percent of my business comes from New York. When a client calls the studio, I just send over my book. Today I can afford to choose only well-paying assignments. When a client pays well, I can spend more time on the artwork. There are people who would call me and say things like, 'Look, we don't have a lot of money, so just do something quick and simple.' Well, that's not the way it works! I can't just pick up a brush and do a few strokes and fax it over!" he says.

It's difficult to give advice on pricing jobs, he says, because everything depends on how badly you need the work and how much the client wants you for the job. "You can consult the price guide prepared by the Graphic Artists Guild, but if you're a young illustrator and don't have a reputation, the clients are going to offer you less, and if you have a big reputation, the clients are willing to pay much more. You have to decide what your work is worth in the marketplace. For example, two years ago, I might have charged four thousand to six thousand dollars for a corporate promotional poster. Today, I can ask for as much as fifteen thousand dollars and some clients are willing to pay for it."

Romero says he wants to be more than an illustrator. In Madrid he was a designer and an art director and he wants his American clients to know that he has these abilities as well. "I'm designing a promotional brochure to show potential clients that I can illustrate, design, and art direct. I did illustrations for magazines because it was the easiest market to get established. Now that I have a reputation, I can expand into other markets and other design disciplines. Some people are happy just doing annual reports, but that's not me. I want to do many things — design toys, games, furniture, restaurants. I see a designer as a creative person who can handle many different types of projects."

Romero has prepared for the future by investing heavily in computers. "Computers will allow me to work for clients all over the world," he says. "For example, we have just finished designing a page for *USA Today* on the computer, and the art work is going to be sent to them over the telephone line. They can get the color separations right on their computer.

"I don't set limits for myself. Some designers say, 'If I make half the money Milton Glaser makes, I'll be satisfied.' But I say, 'Why half? Why not more?'"

Promotional poster for the
Theatre in the Park program in
Queens, New York.

The Autobiography of an Ex-Colored Man

James Weldon Johnson

With a New Introduction by Henry Louis Gates

$7.95/679-72753-1

Book cover for Vintage Books.

## Javier Romero

327 West 21st Street
New York, New York 10011
(212) 206-9175

Illustration and Graphic Design

Clients have included:

Alitalia, American Express, BBDO, Bloomingdale's,
Elizabeth Arden, Foot, Cone & Belding, Fortune, GQ,
Grey Advertising, Hertz, IBM, J. Walter Thompson,
Kenyon Eckhardt, Macy's, Mademoiselle, Nestle, New
York Magazine, Self, Showtime, The New York Times,
Time, Inc., Vanity Fair, Vanguard Records, Wrangler

Works appeared in:

Art Directors Club, 61, 64
Creativity 13, 14, 15
Society of Illustrators 23, 25, 26
Print New York Design
Print Regional Design 84, 85

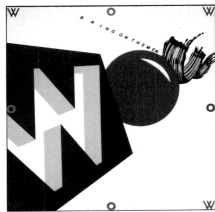

Romero's self-promotional poster.

# Cathleen Toelke

For many years, Cathleen Toelke had no idea what the graphic arts industry was all about. She graduated as an art education major from Buffalo State in the late '60s, but no one had taught her how to make a living with her illustration skills. After college, she worked at many jobs related to the art field. She taught art in public school, worked in her family's wholesale frame shop where she also sold some of her silkscreen designs, and promoted paper for a paper company. During her spare time, she took her portfolio to local agencies and businesses and was paid small sums of money for doing realistic pen-and-ink drawings.

"I was living in Albany, New York, and I had no role model and no information about the commercial arts field. Maybe if I had gone to Parsons or Cooper Union, things would have been different," she explains. During her stint as a paper promoter, she learned more about the graphic arts business and decided to find ways to become a professional illustrator.

"I knew that there were very limited opportunities for an artist in Albany, so I made a decision to move to Boston. I didn't think I could handle a city like New York," she says. "When I first moved to Boston, I didn't think that I knew enough about the business or the town to compete with other professional illustrators, so I got a job at a print shop as a sales rep. I knew that this job would allow me to visit all the agencies and design firms, and it would help me get to know who's who in Boston.

"I also learned a lot of business savvy and confidence, qualities that gave me a definite advantage later on as a freelancer. I was responsible for new business (cold-calling), servicing jobs, and collecting late bills. I learned how to prepare things for print and to spec type."

In Boston, Toelke slowly learned about the business and realized her skills were very much in demand in the advertising world. "I remember I bought a copy of *Communication Arts*, and when I saw all the beautiful graphics in there I finally figured out what the business was all about. Until then, I had no idea how it worked."

When Toelke was given a week's vacation from the print shop, instead of flying straight to Hawaii, she booked portfolio review appointments. "I saw four or five art directors every day. Because I have good technical illustration skills, I got work from small advertising agencies immediately," she says.

Simultaneously, her biggest break came when a well-known art director at Boston's hottest agency, Hill, Holidays, Cosmos & Cosmopulos, liked her work. "He liked the fact that I could really draw, and he gave me full-page newspaper assignments. When I told other art directors that this man was giving me work, they all wanted to see my portfolio. It was like an instant endorsement," she says.

Toelke was also surprised by the amount of money they offered her. "They gave me $650 for my first illustration, which was a lot of money to me in those days. In Albany, I often got paid $15 for a marker sketch for a slide presentation!" she laughs.

But she soon found out that other illustrators were getting even more money. "I bought the pricing guide published by the Graphic Artists Guild and started to quote it as if it was the Bible. So for the second assignment, I asked for $750 and they gave it to me. For the third assignment, I asked for $900 and got it. By the fourth assignment, they were paying me $1,200, then $1,500. I quadrupled my Albany income very quickly," says Toelke.

She spent three years doing realistic pen-and-ink or pencil drawings for advertising agencies. "I just

Illustration for a brochure
promoting the condominium
resort, Village-on-the-Green.

followed the comps; there was very little concept or design involved," she says. She made very good money, but there were also many sleepless nights because of tight agency deadlines.

Toelke was successful working with top agencies because she could produce quality work under tight deadlines. "It wasn't unusual for certain art directors to give me a job at nine o'clock in the morning, and want it by ten o'clock the next morning. I had to stay up all night to get it done. There was just a lot of pressure. People really use you when you're new to the business. There were several occasions where the job was given to me at 5:30 in the evening and the art director would tell me he wanted it by 8:30 the next morning," she recalls.

In 1984, an art director gave her the opportunity to do some full-color illustrations where she was encouraged to come up with her own concept and style. "It pays off to build some very close working relationships with art directors to the point where they can trust you with jobs, even though you may not have a proven track record," she says.

Toelke found that she enjoyed the freedom and the creativity of illustration and began to build a portfolio for color work. In the beginning, she allowed some of her favorite illustrators' styles to heavily influence her illustration, but slowly her own style emerged — realistic, yet painterly, full of rich colors and luscious shapes. "My current style is influenced by a lot of different things, classical and 1920s paintings and sculpture, old Japanese woodcuts, sculptures, and contemporary illustrations," she explains.

The new color portfolio helped her break into the editorial market. Although magazines and books aren't as lucrative as advertising, Toelke says she enjoys the freedom of creating art that's more expressive and personal.

In October 1989, Toelke sold her house in beautiful Cape Cod and moved to Rhinebeck, New York, a lovely town about an hour and a half from New York City. Toelke felt the move would give her better access to the New York publishing, design, and advertising markets.

In 1980, Toelke wasn't ready for New York. But now she comes to town with a list of prestigious clients, including *The New York Times Magazine*, DellaFemina, McNamee, the Boston Museum of Science, and Simon & Schuster. Her work has appeared in prestigious journals from coast to coast, such as Graphis's *Design Annual*, *CA's Illustration Annual*, and the *Print Regional*. She also has a New York rep. What a difference a few years make!

Illustration for a promotional poster for Rand Typography.

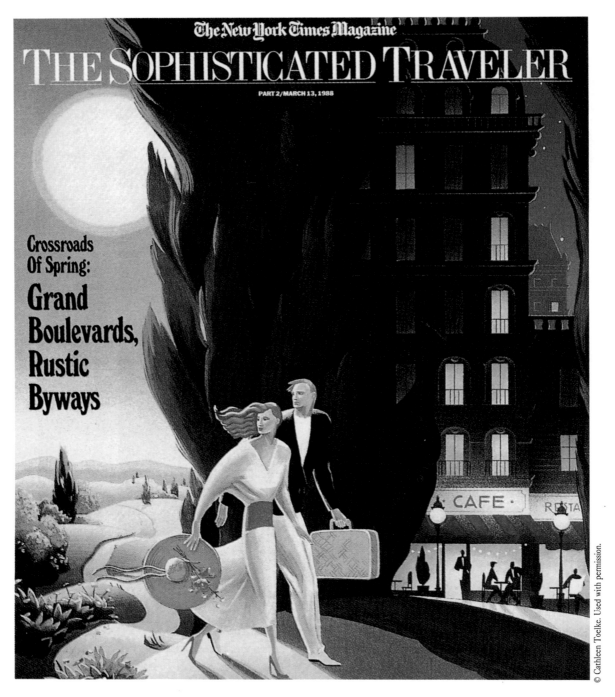

Illustration for the cover of *The Sophisticated Traveler*, a special Sunday magazine edition of *The New York Times*.

Illustration for *Changing Times* magazine.

Cover illustration for "A Real Estate Shopper's Guide," published as a special advertising section in *New York Magazine*.

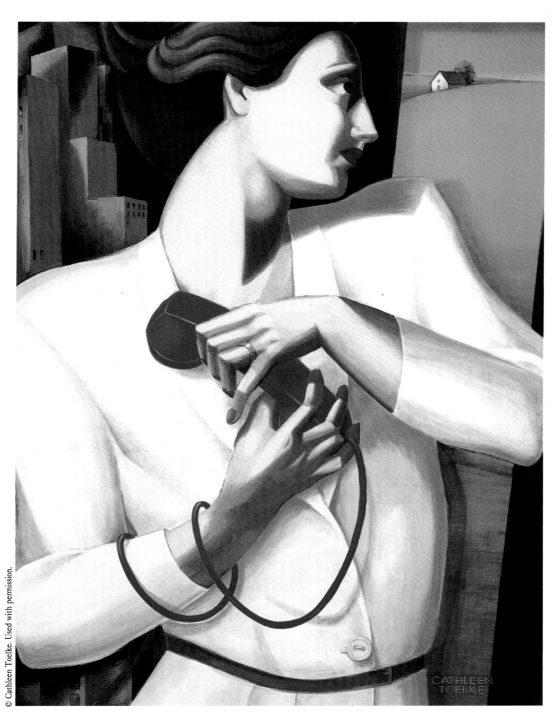

An illustration for *Adweek* magazine.

# *Ty Wilson*

Ty Wilson remembers the first time he negotiated for a job in New York City as if it happened yesterday. It was late January, 1984. He had just arrived in New York from Kansas City. An art director referred him to Yvon Dihe, then the owner of a small upscale advertising agency called L'agency.

Dihe looked through Wilson's fashion portfolio and gave him three big assignments immediately—a billboard, a press kit for a fashion designer, and an invitation to a fashion party at the Puck Building.

Dihe asked Wilson how much he wanted to be paid for the three jobs. Having never worked in New York before, Wilson hadn't the foggiest idea of what to charge. "I wanted to bluff it, but I just kept thinking 'I don't know.'"

"Who am I dealing with, darling?" asked Dihe, in his intimidating French accent. "Am I dealing with a $5 illustrator or a $5,000 illustrator?"

"Well, I guess I'm between $5 and $5,000," replied Wilson.

Seeing that Wilson wasn't used to the game, Dihe threw out some numbers. He said, "Do you want thirty-five or twenty-five?"

Wilson thought, "Well, $35 for an illustration, about $130 for three. If I get six of these assignments a month, I could make rent!" He was about to agree to the price, when Dihe said, "How about fifteen for all three?" Wilson almost said, "Now, wait a minute!" Then he saw Dihe start to scribble numbers on a piece of paper. It was only then that he realized that when Dihe said thirty-five, he meant $350, and when he said fifteen, he really meant $1,500. The original low numbers hadn't seemed strange to Wilson because, in Kansas City, the most he ever got for an illustration was $50! Wilson eventually got $3,500 for the three assignments.

Actually Wilson was doing quite well in Kansas City. He was working for Hallmark, which meant, in Wilson's words, "You can date anybody you want. Hallmark owns half of Kansas City, and you get a great deal of respect for working there," he explains.

He started out in the production department and moved up to the book and calendars department. "I spent four years collecting a nice salary and moaning and groaning about the lack of creativity. Hallmark kept saying they want your ideas, but what they really want is for you to draw little bunnies and little bouquets the Hallmark way," says Wilson. "The money was good, but it's just not the place to be when you want to be young and creative."

Wilson left his job at Hallmark and spent a year freelancing in the Kansas City market. He did illustrations for department stores, but mostly he did paste-up and mechanicals and graphic design. "Art directors really didn't know what to do with my illustrations. I think the style was too sophisticated for that market. I really couldn't sell it." Wilson decided what he really wanted to do was fashion illustration, not graphic design, so he paid a visit to the fashion capital of the world, New York City.

He collected a list of names of art directors he admired and took his portfolio to New York. When he arrived, he called everybody on the list. "I told them, 'I'm from Kansas City and I'm only in town for a week, and can't you please take a look at my book.'" To his surprise, most art directors agreed to see him.

"They were really nice about it. I think they remembered what it was like when they started out. And when I went to see them, I told them I wanted honest opinions. They were very helpful and they gave me concrete comments. Maybe they saw how desperate and scared I really was."

Bob Cole, an art director at Bloomingdale's,

Illustration for a promotional
piece for fashion designer Louis
Feraud.

pointed out to Wilson that he had two distinct styles in his portfolio: one very realistic and safe, and the other strong, bold, and uniquely his own. Cole encouraged Wilson to build a new portfolio that featured his own special style. Wilson also received other advice to show more texture in the clothes and to include more color pieces. Most of the advice was encouraging. Most everybody liked his style and felt that his work only needed some fine-tuning.

Wilson went back to Kansas City encouraged and worked hard on his fashion portfolio. The day after Christmas 1983, he packed up a U-Haul, said adios to his family and sped off to New York with a writer friend. "He was going to be the next Hemingway and I was going to be the next Al Hirschfeld."

"I felt secure in moving, because I felt I had done enough prep work," he recalls. "I had saved enough money to last me a year even if nobody gave me a job. I didn't just come to New York blindly, hoping for the best. I figured I'd give myself a year and if I couldn't make a statement in New York, I'd go back to Kansas City with my tail between my legs and shut up."

Of course, Wilson never had to go back to Kansas City. He has worked for Macy's, Bloomingdale's, *Vogue*, and many prestigious clients. He's been so successful that he's managed to accumulate quite a few horror stories about the business to pass on to others.

"A major department store hired me to do a shopping bag. I did the design and I saw the bag published and got paid for it. A few weeks later, my agent went to the suburbs to shop and found my image plastered all over the New Jersey location of the same department store. They were using it as a major store promotion. It was printed on T-shirts, balloons, and store window pop-ups. My agent knew she hadn't negotiated for that kind of promotional use. I had to call up the department that hired me and complain. They got very nasty about it and insisted that they had negotiated for all those things. This is when you have to make some major decisions about your career. You can either let it go or fight for your money, which is your right. But if you fight, you may never work for them again. The trick is to get compensation and let them save face."

After long negotiations and several letters of complaint, Wilson got some money, but not as much as

he should have gotten. "I got no apologies. But I did save the working relationship and I did work for them again."

Though the fashion market has a reputation for being high-risk in terms of getting paid, Wilson reports that in most cases he has gotten his money. "I'm very professional with my clients. I bill them for thirty days net. If I don't see a check in thirty days, I call accounts receivable and give them my invoice number and the date I sent in the invoice. If I still don't get any response, I'll personally go down to the showroom and sit there until they hand over a check. This tactic has worked for me several times. They really don't want you to sit there, chatting with their receptionist and drinking all their coffee. Of course, the fact that I'm six feet two inches tall helps."

As Wilson got more business, he raised his fees and dropped lower level clients or clients who hadn't been very fair to him. "At different times in your career, you have to make a conscious decision that you're done with one level of clients and you're moving on to the next level," he says.

In the five years Wilson has been in New York, he has had two good years, one great year, and one excruciatingly slow year. "There was this one year when I just thought everybody had forgotten me."

Sensing that putting all his eggs in one basket was dangerous, Wilson used the slow times to develop a new portfolio for other markets. "I used the same elegant line style, but I did images that weren't fashion oriented."

With the new portfolio, Wilson got work illustrating two theater posters for Broadway plays. He also hired a rep to help him develop new markets for his work. His rep sent some of his brochures to a poster publisher and he negotiated a contract to produce six poster designs. The posters are on sale across the country at hundreds of retail poster shops and Wilson is now collecting royalties. Since the posters sold well, Wilson's rep has encouraged Wilson to put these designs on T-shirts, and she is now developing marketing strategies for the T-shirts.

Wilson strongly feels that, in order to stay afloat in this competitive business, artists today must learn to diversify and develop new markets for their work.

Decorative poster for Judy
Nidermaier, a designer of store
display fixtures.

One of a series of decorative
retail wall posters published by
Bruce McGaw Graphics in New
York City.

Caricature of Brooke Shields for
*Seventeen* magazine.

Advertising illustration for
fashion designer Albert Nipon.

Another wall poster published
by Bruce McGaw Graphics.

# Lane Smith

Lane Smith grew up in Southern California and attended the Art Center in Pasadena. He graduated in 1983, a year after his schoolmates, illustrators Matt Mahurin and Greg Spalenka. Like his friends, Smith came East to seek his fame and fortune and was quite successful at it.

Since his arrival in New York City in 1984, Smith's painterly images have appeared in many major publications, including *Esquire*, *Rolling Stone*, *Texas Monthly*, and the *New York Times*. He has also illustrated three critically acclaimed children's books, *Halloween ABC*, *Flying Jake* and *The True Story of the Three Little Pigs*. *Halloween ABC* was named by the *New York Times* as one of the ten best illustrated children's books of 1987.

Smith came to New York with a student portfolio full of black-and-white, New Wave charcoal drawings. He went about seeking work aggressively, making appointments with art directors all over town. "One of the art directors at the *New York Times* told me that my work was too stylized for the *Times*, but I convinced her to give me a chance," says Smith. She gave him a spot drawing for the paper's editorial section, and was so delighted with Smith's piece that she gave him a daily assignment for an entire week.

An art director at BBDO (an advertising agency) spotted Smith's drawings in the *Times* and hired him to do a print advertising campaign for a television program for PBS. "The *New York Times* is a great place to get exposure, so many people read it," comments Smith. BBDO paid him a thousand dollars for each full-page illustration. It wasn't very much money for advertising, but this was Smith's first major assignment and it made him feel more confident about his future in New York. "I came here with only $1,500 in my pocket. I spent the first five weeks sleeping on Matt Mahurin's floor," he says, laughing at those salad days.

Though Smith got a couple of lucky breaks during his first few weeks in New York, he soon discovered that his New Wave style illustration was not very marketable.

"The work was too stylized, some people were calling it 'post punk.' It looked kind of rebellious and threatening; not many mainstream publications could use it," he explains.

During the first year, Smith picked up just enough assignments to pay the rent. With time on his hands, he began to explore other styles and techniques. "I finally learned to paint. At the Art Center I got bad grades early on because I couldn't paint." In New York, Smith painted every day. Most of his subjects evolved around playful imagery from his childhood. He developed a new painterly style that relied more on textures and color, yet retained the haunting beauty that was exhibited in his black-and-white charcoal drawings.

Within a year, Smith had created thirty small paintings, most of which used scary images incorporating the alphabet. A friend who was an art director saw them and suggested he show them to a children's book publisher. Smith took his original paintings to Macmillan, a major New York publishing firm.

An editor there liked the paintings so much that she teamed him up with established children's book writer, Eve Merriam. Smith was given a contract and six months to complete *Halloween ABC*.

"The traditional way to land a children's book contract for a beginner is to write the manuscript, make a dummy of the book, lay out a finished spread, then present it to a publisher," he says. "I did it a little differently. I showed a series of

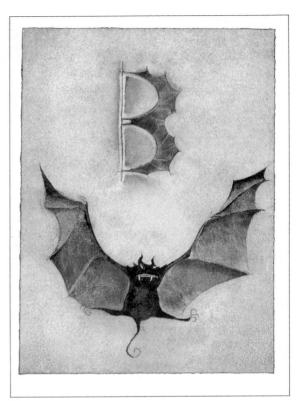

Pages from Smith's first children's book, *Halloween ABC*.

original paintings, they liked the paintings, and then found me a writer."

Smith says a typical book contract for a first-time illustrator offers an advance against royalties of anywhere from four thousand to eight thousand dollars. "The publisher gives you half up front, and the other half after you complete the book. Then they send you your share of the royalties every six months. The royalty is usually 5 to 10 percent of the profit. The theory is, if your first two books sell well, you can then negotiate for more lucrative contracts."

Smith now has an agent to handle his book deals. His second book, *Flying Jake* was published by Macmillan. But his third book, *The True Story of the Three Little Pigs*, written by Jon Scieszka, was published by Viking, another New York publishing house.

For Smith, illustrating books is a labor of love. "It's great to see thirty of your paintings in one place, but it's also a financial sacrifice for me since I have to turn down a lot of editorial assignments while I'm working on a book. For example, a full-page illustration in *Esquire* can pay as much as two thousand dollars, while a book which contains thirty to forty full-color illustrations will only pay an advance of several thousand dollars."

Breaking into the editorial and children's book market is only the beginning for this ambitious illustrator. Smith is now busy working on a personal animation project. "While I was a student at the Art Center, I made an animation film, and it made it to the semifinals in the student category of the Academy Awards. Now I want to do a personal piece, something that I can enter in film festivals. Hopefully, someone will see it and offer me an opportunity to direct animation films," Smith explains.

To make it in this business, says Smith, all you need is talent and perseverence. "The quality of your work gets better the longer you work at it. And the work will get easier. Projects that used to take three or four days to complete now take me only one day."

A high-energy illustration for
the children's book, *Flying Jake*.

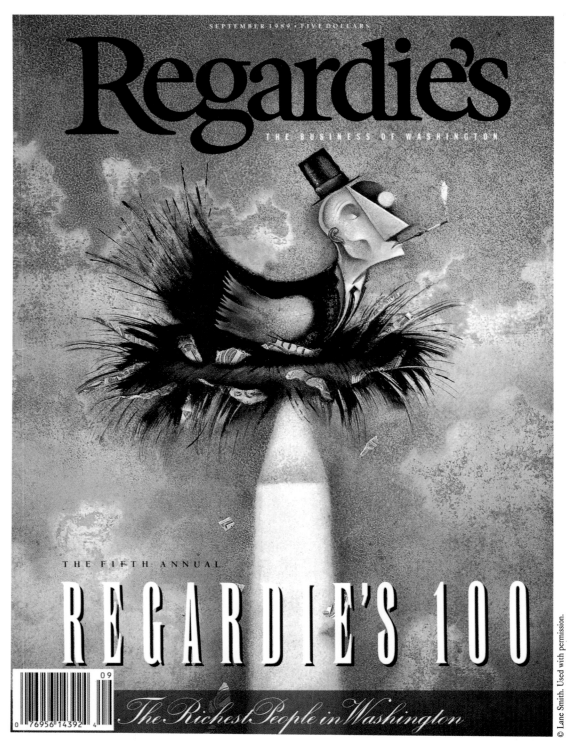

Cover illustration for *Regardie's*,
a business magazine headquar-
tered in Washington, D.C.

A colorful page for *Rolling Stone*,
illustrating an article on dreams.

# Brian Ajhar

"I never had any doubt that I was going to make a living in art," says Brian Ajhar. "While I was at Parsons, the teachers would advise us to take mechanical classes, just in case we couldn't make it in illustration. I never took those classes because I was determined to be an illustrator."

A year before he graduated from Parsons, Ajhar took his portfolio to New York art directors, just to get feedback on his work. "I called up about thirty art directors on the phone and said, 'Hi, I'm a student at Parsons. I'm not ready to take on assignments yet, but I would like to show you my book and get some advice on my work.' Most people were very nice about it and gave me an appointment. I think people took the time to see me because I wasn't asking for work, just advice."

At the time, Ajhar had many different styles in his portfolio. He included work from all his illustration classes, including oil paintings, watercolor pieces, and etchings. "They liked my work a lot, but they all said I needed to choose a direction—there were too many different styles in the portfolio."

Ajhar was very encouraged by the art directors response to his work. Many of them told him to come back to see them after he graduated.

He also took his book to galleries, and they offered to put him on their waiting list. "I didn't want to wait five years before I could make a living," says Ajhar. "So I dropped the idea of being a gallery artist and concentrated on my illustration work."

After graduation in 1980, he took a two-month vacation in Europe and then came back to New York to beat the pavement. His first assignment came quickly, from art director Will Hopkins, who asked him to do a two-page spread for *Horizon* magazine. "The fee was low (two hundred dollars), but I needed the printed tearsheet. I was very anxious about the job because it was my first assignment. I really overworked the piece. It got printed, but it wasn't something I wanted to put in my portfolio. My advice to young illustrators is, don't try to put everything you learn into your first job. Just relax and do the best you can," says Ajhar.

Ajhar got work quickly because he had a good portfolio, and he went after work aggressively, making cold calls every day.

"Some of my friends didn't get work for a couple of years after they graduated, because they weren't ready to deal with clients. They had a couple of bad experiences and just gave up looking. They ended up waiting on tables or selling art supplies. What a waste of talent! I tried not to get discouraged. I was always showing my books around."

Early on, Ajhar got work from a variety of magazines, including *McCall's*, *Working Mother*, *Dun's Business Month*, and *American Photographer*. After about a year into the business, it was clear to him that his most marketable pieces were illustrations that have a sense of humor.

"The humor pieces really took off. People seemed to like my pencil and watercolor illustrations because they're more painterly than the standard comic cartoons. The caricatures and concepts have a satirical edge."

The style, witty and sophisticated, was perfect for business publications, and soon Ajhar was working for *Business Week*, *Money* magazine, and *Forbes*, all of which paid much better than fashion magazines. In 1989, Ajhar received an average of two thousand dollars for covers and four hundred to six hundred dollars for spot illustrations.

As his reputation grew, his illustrations also appeared in *Sports Illustrated*, *Lear*, *Time*, and *Rolling Stone*. In 1987, Ajhar billed a total of ninety-seven

Illustration for a book jacket for
*Hollywood Anecdotes*, published
by William Morrow.

jobs. He estimated that he had to turn down about thirty assignments. "I'm busy enough that I try not to take less than a thousand dollars for a full-page illustration, and not less than six hundred dollars for a spot illustration." Of course, like most artists, Ajhar makes exceptions, "I am willing to charge less for a magazine like *Utne Reader*, because it's a publication I really like, and I know they don't have a big budget. And if I do a cover for them I know the magazine will be on the newsstand for two months, and that's good exposure for me."

There are several reasons why Ajhar gets so much work. His classical illustration style can easily fit into any magazine or newspaper, and the concepts are clever and sophisticated, yet not obscure or difficult to understand. The illustrations complement the text without distracting the serious reader. Ajhar also has a reputation for working fast. He often gets two- to three-day deadlines from desperate art directors who need the work yesterday! His pencil and watercolor techniques allow him to work very fast. Ajhar points out that he is always under pressure to get the work out. "There are many times when I don't get any sleep," he says.

Ajhar has done advertising work, but he prefers editorial assignments because they usually allow him more creative freedom. "In advertising, you usually have to follow a tight comp, you don't get to come up with your own concept," he explains. He points out that creative freedom has to be earned. "You have to show the art director you are capable of thinking on the very first assignment. Otherwise, he'll get used to dictating his concepts to you."

What does he do if an art director gives him a concept that he's not crazy about? "Well, I don't say, 'This concept stinks,' " he laughs. "I'll probably say something like, 'Let me play around with it and I'll see what I can come up with.' I'll try to come up with several different concepts and hope they choose the best one."

Although Ajhar enjoys working with pencil and watercolor, he says that his goal is to develop a style where he can incorporate the many different techniques he has learned in the past.

"I'm building a house in the country and that'll give me the space I need to experiment with different styles and techniques," he says. It looks like Ajhar's most creative work may be yet to come.

Ajhar captures the mood of the Tyson-Givens marital match in this full-page illustration for *Rolling Stone's* year-end special issue.

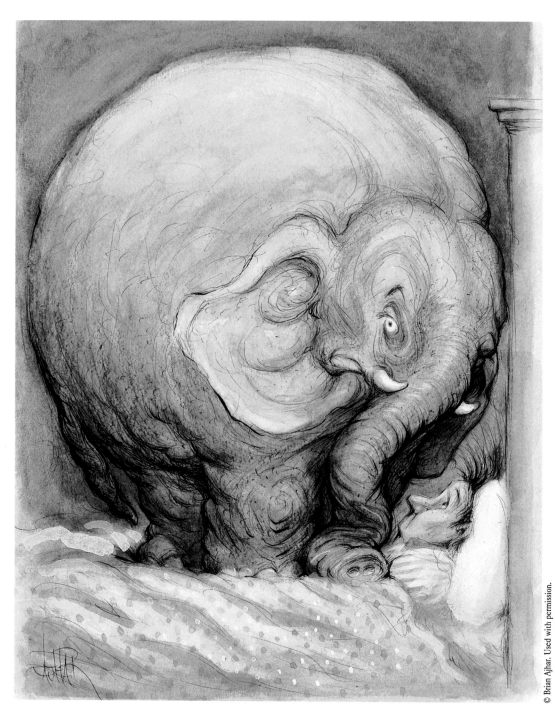

Illustration for an article on the "Heart Attack Elephant" that appeared in a prototype of a magazine designed by Steve Philips Design.

Illustration for *Investment Guide*,
a special advertising section in
*New York* magazine.

# David Diaz

David Diaz grew up in Fort Lauderdale, Florida, and received his formal art education at the Fort Lauderdale Art Institute. Like most ambitious young artists, Diaz paid a visit to New York City soon after he graduated from college. But having lived in the Sunshine state all his life, Diaz found New York's struggling artists scene not very enticing. So he and his girlfriend settled in beautiful San Diego.

"When I got to San Diego in 1979, I took any job I could get. I did a lot of paste-up and graphic design. And occasionally, I sold illustrations to local newspapers like the *San Diego Reader*, a weekly art and entertainment newspaper," he says.

Although Diaz's first love is illustration, he could hardly live on the twenty-five dollar fees that the local papers were paying him. So he ended up spending most of his time doing mechanicals and graphic design for publishing companies. "In those days, San Diego's pay rate for illustration was much lower than L.A.'s," he comments. "There is really no justification for this, since the cost of living here is just as expensive as L.A."

However, Diaz points out that San Diego has developed into a very sophisticated city, and prices today are more in line with rest of the country than ten years ago.

In 1984, five years after he arrived in California, Diaz decided to make a conscious effort to get more illustration work. "Before that, I was just taking on any assignments that came along, and most of them were graphic design work. But what I really wanted to do was illustration. I didn't want to wake up twenty years from now regretting that I never even tried to be an accomplished illustrator."

Though Diaz had a portfolio full of high-quality illustrations, he had not formulated a personal style that he could market as his own. "Most of my early work was realistic pen-and-ink drawings; they have a very graphic feel, but not something that can be defined as a 'style.' "

Diaz knew that to make a name for himself, he had to develop a more personal vision. "During one of my visits to New York, in the late '70s, I saw an exhibit of German Expressionist paintings at the Guggenheim Museum. I was very inspired by the graphic style of the paintings, and I experimented with a new style that uses the paintings in this show as a major influence. My technique loosened up. The earlier work I did was very tight, and I often relied on photographs and reference materials. As I experimented with different techniques and styles, I developed a more intuitive drawing style. I stopped using reference materials, and relied more on my own imagination."

As a result of his experimentation and exploration, Diaz developed two distinct styles using the scratchboard technique—a playful woodcut style, with a sophisticated cubist look, and a paper cut-out style with sharp edges, resulting in a crude, primitive look.

There is a charming, playful quality to the style that has turned out to be successful and versatile in the marketplace. By combining different shapes and colors, Diaz can get different effects. It can look abstract and intellectual, which is great for book covers and magazine work, or by using bright saturated colors, it can look charming and decorative, which is perfect for upscale promotional materials.

The new portfolio took Diaz nearly two years to complete. Once he was happy with his new collection of work, he wanted to show it off in a beautiful promotional brochure. "I had two hundred and fifty booklets printed in four colors. The illustrations were printed on beautiful Japanese textured paper.

Illustration published in
*The San Diego Union.*

and each book was handbound by my wife. I wanted to create a piece so beautiful that it wouldn't end up in the trash," Diaz explains.

And his efforts paid off. Two years after he sent out the promotional piece, he still gets calls for work from people who received the brochure. "I think people just keep it around and when they have a project that's right for me, they call," he says.

The brochure also gave Diaz a lot of priceless free publicity. It was published in *Print Regional* and *American Illustration*, won a silver medal from the New York Art Director's Club, and got into the AIGA show. "I sent out about fifty copies to New York art directors. I got very good responses from New York, and it was only the first time I attempted to get work outside of San Diego," says Diaz.

His new style turned out to be a hit with art directors across the country. His work was published in *Self*, *The Atlantic Monthly*, *The Washington Post*, and *Vogue's* new rival, *Mirabella*. He has also illustrated a series of book covers for Harper & Row.

Today, Diaz only takes on design work he finds challenging. Most of his time is spent illustrating for clients across the country. For Diaz, there will be no regrets when it comes time to look back on the decisions he made for his career.

Book cover for the novel, *Tell My Horse*.

# Nancy Skolos

Nancy Skolos started out in life wanting to be a professional clarinetist. During her senior year in high school, she auditioned for Oberlin Conservatory, Indiana University, and the University of Cincinnati. She was living in Lima, Ohio, at the time and didn't want to be too far away from home.

One day after school she found two rejection letters in her mailbox, "I ran into the house, played a Mozart concerto on the stereo, and sobbed into the carpet." When Skolos finished mourning her losses, she got on the phone to the University of Cincinnati, the only school she hadn't heard from, and transferred her school records to the design department. "I didn't want to read another rejection letter," she explained. "My father was an industrial designer, and that's a field I thought I could always fall back on."

Skolos spent two years studying industrial design at the University of Cincinnati before she discovered that what she really wanted to be was a graphic designer, so she transferred to the Cranbrook Academy of Art. "I had heard that Cranbrook had a free and creative environment and didn't have formal classes or give grades and thought, 'Boy, that's the school for me!' "

At Cranbrook, students were encouraged to experiment with different styles and techniques. And the school put a heavy emphasis on conceptual design. Skolos felt at home there. "They allow you to develop your own creative vision in a very creative, design-oriented environment." Cranbrook infused Skolos with the idea that art is more than an image on a piece of paper, that it should be incorporated into everyday life. "Everything we did at Cranbrook was a design experience — eating lunch was a design experience," she recalls.

After Cranbrook, Skolos went on to graduate school at Yale University's School of Art where she studied art history and the history of typography. At that time, Skolos didn't think about being the best designer in the world. "I just wanted to find a job and be a good worker. But now that I think back on it, I think I was more ambitious than I had realized. I remember once some IBM recruiters came to Yale to interview graduate students, and they went through my portfolio and asked if I expected to be famous someday, and I said 'Yeah, it shouldn't be too hard, there isn't much good design work being done right now.' I was only kidding, but they didn't hire me. Who wants to deal with an ego like that?"

After graduation, Skolos got a job with a "moody designer who screamed and yelled a lot." The experience was so traumatic that Skolos thought she could never work for another employer again, so she teamed up with her husband, professional photographer Thomas Wedell, and their Cranbrook schoolmate Ken Raynor, and started a design studio called Skolos, Wedell + Raynor. It was 1980; Skolos had only been out of school for a year.

"If that horrible experience hadn't happened to me, I don't think I would have started my own place," she confesses.

In the beginning, it was a "real seat-of-the-pants operation." Skolos enlisted help from her old friends from Cranbrook and got some referrals. She even looked up help wanted ads in Boston newspapers, searching for startup businesses. "I found these ads that said, 'New company looking for sales rep,' and I figured if it's a new company, maybe they'll need a graphic designer. I actually got a few jobs that way. There was this ad that said, 'Exciting Journalistic Enterprise looking for advertising sales rep.' So I called the number and asked, 'Hi, is this the Exciting Journalistic Enterprise?" And the guy on the

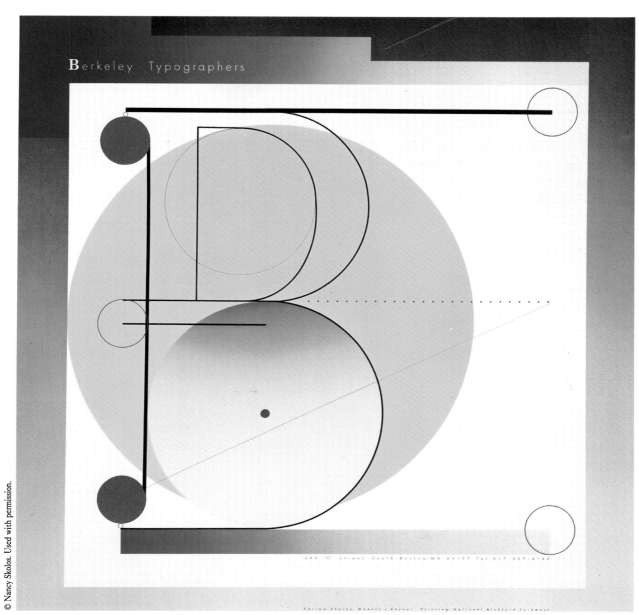

Poster for Berkeley Typographers.

other end said, 'I guess so.' And I said, 'Do you need an art director?' And he asked, 'What's an art director?' So I explained it to him. He gave me an interview, and I got the job. We designed the very first issue of *Sportscape* magazine. You really have to have a good sense of humor in order to live through the early desperate days!"

At the start, pricing jobs was a major headache for Skolos. "I didn't know what to charge, and I had to call other designer friends for help. There are a lot of companies in Boston that use young designers and pay them a lot less than they're worth. I've designed book covers for three hundred dollars and promotional brochures for two hundred dollars. I used to get very emotional about doing the billing because I felt like I was taking money from poor people or something. But now, it's just mathematics. I don't get emotional about it anymore."

Within a few short years, Skolos, Wedell + Raynor was working for major computer companies such as Wang and Digital. "The high-tech companies were flourishing in Boston in the early '80s and our modern geometric style conveyed the abstract concepts behind those high-tech software products," Skolos explains.

Not only did the firm achieve financial success, the designs won local and national awards, and several corporate promotional posters were curated as part of the permanent collections at The Museum of Modern Art and The Metropolitan Museum of Art.

Skolos attributes the work's critical success to the three partners' formal art training at Cranbrook. "The three of us share an interest in the history of modern art, and we incorporate a lot of the philosophies and techniques from various modern art movements into our graphic design, including Surrealism, Cubism, and Constructivism."

Winning awards has earned the studio an upscale reputation. But Skolos finds this honor both a blessing and a curse. "The good thing is, it attracts clients who appreciate good design. But on the negative side, it scares away many bread-and-butter clients who automatically assume that we're too expensive. So we have to constantly remind people that we may be good, but we're not that much more expensive than our competitors."

Since 1980, Skolos, Wedell + Raynor has grown from a three-person firm to a ten-person firm. But Skolos says growth in the high-tech business in Boston has slowed down quite a bit, and she has been pitching design services to clients in different parts of the country. "Even after nine years in the business, I'm still very insecure about the financial aspects of the business. I feel like it can all be over tomorrow."

Despite business concerns, Skolos remains an idealistic designer who believes beautiful graphic design, whether it's hung in the Museum of Modern Art or printed on a detergent box, plays an important role in enriching the lives of the people. "I like the idea of doing good design for the masses," she says.

Poster to promote a printer's
new scanner.

# Marcus Von Nispel

In Frankfurt, Germany, Marcus Von Nispel was considered something of a boy wonder in the advertising industry. He started working in an ad agency when he was fifteen, and by seventeen he was winning awards for his campaigns. At the ripe old age of twenty, he had worked for nine different advertising agencies. "I moved around a lot because I found that people always saw you as the kid they hired, even though you'd learned a great deal in a few months and were ready to take on more important projects," he explains. In 1984, when he was twenty, Von Nispel felt that he was ready for America, where all the great music videos and commercials were being produced.

"In Germany, we don't have big production budgets, so you can't design commercials with great special effects or expensive sets," he says.

Von Nispel obtained a Fulbright scholarship to study computer graphics in New York. "The truth was, I had only a minor interest in computer graphics. I always thought I was technophobic, but in order to get the Fulbright scholarship, you have to say you want to study something you can't study in your own country."

His plan was to get a job as art director at a big agency in New York City the moment he arrived. "I thought it would be easy because I did such good work in Frankfurt, but it turned out not to be the case." His first interview was with one of the largest agencies, Young and Rubicam (Y&R). "I walked into this big room and there were hundreds of portfolios piled up against the wall. The interviewer told me that in the summer Y&R gets hundreds of portfolios and résumés a day from designers and art directors from all over the world."

Although Von Nispel had worked at the Frankfurt division of Y&R, the New York office didn't offer him a job right away. So he took his book to all the major advertising agencies, including Ogilvy & Mather, Ted Bates, and J. Walter Thompson. "I had a list of sixty people I wanted to see, and every day I would call these people and make appointments to show my book. At J. Walter Thompson, everybody said they liked my book, but nobody wanted to take responsibility for hiring me because I didn't have working papers. So everybody kept referring me to someone else. I must have dropped off my book there thirty or forty times. There were times when I didn't know if anybody even opened it up. I used to clip a piece of thread to the zipper and, if the thread was gone, I knew someone had looked at it. Once, I found cigar ashes in my book, and that got me all excited. I thought someone important must have looked at it!"

Von Nispel eventually got freelance assignments from Bates and J. Walter Thompson, and a few months later was hired as an art director at Y&R.

How he got into the entertainment business sounds like a Hollywood fairy tale. He heard that famous art director Steven Frankfurt was giving a talk at the Art Directors Club. "He was my idol. I used to read all about him in magazines like *Adweek* and *Ad Age*," he says.

"At that time, the Art Directors Club met in a penthouse apartment in midtown Manhattan. I went there but I didn't know anybody. So I walked out onto the balcony and saw all these beautiful penthouse apartments down below, and I thought, 'Wow! This is the American dream!' Suddenly there was this man in a suit standing next to me, and he pointed to an apartment across the way and said, 'I want to move over there, the one with the swimming pool.'" And I said, 'Okay, let's share!'

That was the frame of mind I was in. I was living in a horrible place in Brooklyn and I couldn't imag-

Poster for the annual film
festival sponsored by Robert
Redford's Sundance Institute.

ine having a big penthouse to myself. I had to share it! The man in the suit said, 'Why are you here?' I said, 'Oh, I work for Y&R.' and he said, 'I used to work for Y&R. I notice you have an accent, where are you from?' I said, 'Frankfurt.' And he said, "That's funny. My name is Frankfurt," and I just went, 'Oh, my God!' "

Well, in the course of the conversation, Frankfurt found out that Von Nispel was studying computer graphics and arranged for him to show his portfolio and reel to his son Peter who was working for R/Greenberg Associates, a graphic design and film production company.

Not long after that, R/Greenberg called and asked Von Nispel, "How would you like to work for Steven Spielberg?" Needless to say, Von Nispel jumped at the opportunity. The project was *The Money Pit*, starring Tom Hanks. Von Nispel designed the credits, logos, posters, trailers, animation, commercials, and the music video. "Getting the big break has a lot to do with luck, but you can increase your chances by going out and meeting lots of people," he says.

At R/Greenberg, Von Nispel worked as a conceptual designer where he developed visual concepts for corporate logo animations, music videos, and movie trailers. "I came up with the concept and design, sketched out the storyboard, and a large pool of technicians would bring it to life on the screen," he explains.

Some of his most memorable jobs include work on *Star Trek*, *Dirty Dancing*, a music video for rock singer Robert Plant, and a computer-generated logo for General Motors.

While he was at R/Greenberg, he took on freelance assignments for Portfolio, a design firm he started with film producer Anouk Frankel. In 1988, he left R/Greenberg to devote all his energy to building up Portfolio. "It's a full-service graphic design and film production company. For example, for a movie project we can do everything from film to print. We can do the credit trailers, the TV commercial, the promotional poster, and any project that promotes the movie. The same goes for TV programs, music, and advertising."

Von Nispel says that he hopes that by managing his own company, he'll be able to devote more time to interesting projects and have more control over the entire creative process.

Von Nispel art directed this
elegant black-and-white music
video for singers Ashford and
Simpson.

# Laurie Rosenwald

Laurie Rosenwald gets to do all the fun stuff—a record album cover for Warner Brothers, shopping bags for Bloomingdale's and Fiorucci, a set of plates for Shiseido, a Japanese company, and . . .

"I never give anybody any indication that I want to do boring projects. When people call me, they call me to do something that will make a splash, something that jumps up and grabs people's eyeballs," Rosenwald explains. Indeed, every piece in her portfolio is eye catching. The bold shapes and colors in her design generate energy without being loud and obvious.

Rosenwald has been working as a freelance designer/illustrator for twelve years. She was a fine arts major at the Rhode Island School of Design, but she loved graphic design and took many design electives. After she graduated in 1976, she went back to New York, looking for work as an illustrator. "I didn't have any connections, so I just made a lot of cold calls. I saw Milton Glaser, Seymour Chwast, and many other art directors. Everybody told me that my work was too personal for the commercial market."

Not having the faintest idea what an illustration portfolio should look like, Rosenwald went around town carrying a huge portfolio full of 30 × 40-inch white ink on black paper drawings. "They were drawings I did for my painting, very abstract and complex, not at all right for the commercial market," she recalls.

One fateful day, Rosenwald dragged her portfolio to the *New York Times*. While the art director went through her drawings, Rosenwald became desperate and blurted out, "Oh, by the way, I do mechanicals."

It was a dangerous statement, since Rosenwald had never done a mechanical in her life. "Not only had I never done one, I didn't even know what the word meant. I just heard people say you can make money doing it," she laughs.

The *Times* called that very afternoon, asking Rosenwald to report to work the next day. "I ran out to the bookstore and bought a how-to book on mechanicals. I didn't understand a word of it."

The next day, Rosenwald bravely showed up for work. Someone led her to a drafting table. "There was a round plastic thing sitting on the table, so I picked it up and asked the guy sitting next to me, 'What is this?' Suddenly everybody in the room looked up, and I could hear them thinking, 'Oh my God, this girl doesn't know a damn thing!' "

The little round plastic thing turned out to be a proportion wheel. But instead of chasing Rosenwald out the door, the art staff admired her gutsy personality and took her under their wings and taught her layout and paste-up.

Rosenwald freelanced at the *Times* for about a year, and learned a great deal about newspaper design. With the connections she made at the country's most important newspaper, she found work designing for *Self* and illustrating for *Vanity Fair*.

In 1979, she took a job as an assistant to a famous fashion illustrator, the late Antonio Lopez. "I did everything from deliveries to buying paper. We had a great time. It was the disco era, we would work all day and dance all night at clubs like Studio 54," recalls Rosenwald.

Around this time, Rosenwald made connections with upscale fashion clients, including European and Japanese companies. She designed window displays, T-shirts, stationery for Fiorucci, shopping bags for Bloomingdale's, and ads for Issey Miyake that appeared in *Vogue*. In 1980 she followed Fiorucci to Milan, Italy. While there, she showed her portfolio to Condé Nast and ended up doing pages

Poster promoting the tour of
French pop singer France Gall.

for *Vogue*, *Cosmo*, and other Condé Nast publications.

"In Paris, the art directors went cuckoo bananas over my work. They were very receptive to my style. In Europe, I get advertising assignments, but almost never in the U.S. American advertisers still prefer realistic illustrations. Realism is an American tradition, like Norman Rockwell or Andrew Wyeth. The Europeans are more *avant garde*. After all, it is easy to forget that modern art comes from Europe and *avant garde* is a French word."

How does one get work in Paris and Milan? "The same way you do it in the U.S. You take your portfolio to all the art directors. It helps if you can speak some Italian or French," says Rosenwald.

Though it's fun to travel and work all over the world, Rosenwald warns it's not always easy to re-establish yourself with your clients when you're back in town. "If you saw the hundreds of names in my appointment book after a long trip, it would break your heart," she says. "I'm always searching for the most interesting clients. Those that really want originality and are willing to take a little risk."

Rosenwald is certain that by freelancing and not establishing a design studio, she has traded in financial rewards for personal and creative freedom. "I've traveled all over the world, and I used to take off two months every summer to paint, but I don't have a house in the country or fancy cars like some of my friends. But I'm sure that, in order to maintain that kind of lifestyle, they have to take on a lot of jobs. They do it just for the money, things I believe they don't find interesting. But being by myself, by not having overhead expenses, I can afford to say 'no' to projects that are not right for me. That's the luxury in my lifestyle."

However, after twelve years of working alone in her loft, Rosenwald recently rented an office in a space shared by several individual designers. "We're sharing rent and office equipment. It's hard to work alone. You have to handle every phone call and hang around the house all day for deliveries."

Rosenwald has also designed a splashy major self-promotional piece explaining to potential clients all her creative abilities as designer and illustrator. And with a client list that includes Condé Nast, Bloomingdale's, Bergdorf Goodman, Fiorucci, the Paris Metro, and Warner Brothers Records, how could she lose?

"I never feel like I have a career. I feel like I have an interesting life. I haven't always made the easiest choices, but I've made the most creative ones," says Rosenwald.

Promotional poster for the one
hundredth birthday celebration
of the Eiffel Tower.

An illustration for a promotional
booklet for IBM.

A set of whimsical plates for a
Japanese company, Shiseido.

# *Tom Antista*

Looking at Tom Antista's successful career today, it's hard to imagine that at one time his alma mater, the University of Utah, didn't think he had what it takes to be a graphic designer. "I didn't put a lot of effort into my school work during my first semester as a design major there, and they asked me to choose another major." Instead of taking the school's recommendation, Antista became obsessed with the idea of becoming a great designer. Three years later, he graduated at the top of his class.

During his senior year, Antista decided to strengthen his student portfolio with published work to gain a competitive edge. "I volunteered my services to anybody who would allow me to do creative work. I went to all the different departments in my school and offered to do design pieces for them. I worked at the design department of the school's television station. I found a magazine in town, and I offered to do the covers for them at nominal fees if they would let me do creative work. By the time I graduated, I had a portfolio that showed that I had a lot of working experience," explains Antista.

Antista graduated in 1982. "The graduation took place on a Saturday, and that following Monday, I was on a plane to San Francisco looking for a job." Antista wanted to work in San Francisco because there were a lot of designers there that he admired. "The way I saw it, Los Angeles has a lot of famous design studios and San Francisco has a lot of famous designers. I wanted to be a great designer. At that time, my first choice was San Francisco, my second was L.A., and New York, my third."

The young graduate spent a week in the city by the bay, showing his portfolio to various design firms. "They all liked the portfolio and gave me valuable advice, but I didn't get any job offers." On Friday he flew back home, spent the weekend in Salt Lake City, and by Monday he was on the plane again, this time to Los Angeles.

He spent the week showing his portfolio around. On Friday, he showed it to designer James Cross, of James Cross Associates. "He liked the portfolio, but he did mostly annual reports, and I didn't have any annual report experience, but he said he knew of someone who had just broken up with his partner and was looking for a designer; he could set up an appointment for me on Monday. So I explained, 'It's now one o'clock, my plane leaves at five. Can you please get me an appointment today?'" Cross, being a gentleman, got on the phone and got Antista an interview with design firm owner Rusty Kay. Three weeks later, Kay gave Antista the job. "I offered to take the job for a minimum salary. He couldn't pass up such an offer. I just wanted the opportunity to work in Los Angeles."

Antista spent three and a half years at Rusty Kay's, doing a variety of projects, including brochures, logos, packaging, and catalogs. Most of the work was not very glamorous, but Rusty Kay invented great promotional projects for Antista. "I created beautiful promotional posters for the studio. These silkscreen posters won design awards and put us on the map as a design studio. After a while, I started building a reputation around town, and people started to give me freelance work."

At Rusty Kay's, Antista learned to do design at a fast pace. "The senior designer he hired never came on board, so I ended up being the only designer in the studio. He brought in the clients and managed the business, and I did all the designing and production. When things got too busy, we hired freelance help. But most of the time, it was just me working away."

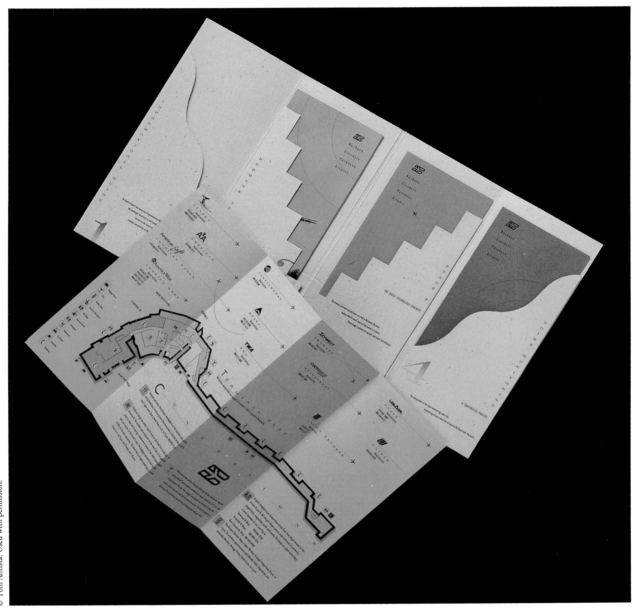

Antista designed this information guide for Burbank's
Glendale Pasadena Airport.

Three and a half years later, Antista felt it was time to move on. "I was making a good salary, but I knew that a partnership was not in the cards. And I found the freelance work I got was more exciting than what the studio was doing. So I decided to start my own firm."

So Antista left Rusty Kay. He leased an office and opened Antista Design. "It was the scariest thing I've ever done, but it was also the most exciting thing I've ever done," he recalls. He made a lot of cold calls, targeting construction firms, hospitals, furniture companies, and any business that might provide him with ongoing design projects.

Antista found that vendors in L.A. were very supportive of young designers starting their own business. "If they think you have real talent, the typesetters and the printers will give you a head start by giving you credit," he says.

Antista Design has promoted the studio by winning design competitions. His elaborate self-promotional posters have gotten him into various design publications, including *Communication Arts*, *Print*, and *HOW*. "If you're a young designer, this is the fastest way to let people know who you are," he explains.

The business grew quickly. Two years later he had a staff of four, and three years later he had a staff of eight and was billing about $800,000 a year. "As the business grew by leaps and bounds, I hired more people than I could effectively manage. There was a large overhead, which took a lot of work to keep fueled," Antista admits candidly. But as his business accounts changed, the scope and the goals of the studio changed, too. In 1989, Antista returned the business to its original setup, which was just himself as designer and a business manager.

"Before, with a staff of seven, I never had enough time to design. I had meetings all day long in and out of the studio. Now I am more selective about my clients and am able to spend more time on creative projects that help build my reputation," explains Antista.

Instead of emphasizing growth of the studio, says Antista, he is looking forward to growing as a designer. His dream of being one of the best designers is still very much alive.

Handsome packaging for
Wolfgang Pizza (owned by celebrity chef Wolfgang Puck)
that was designed by Antista.

# A Word from Art Directors

JUDY GARLAN
*The Atlantic Monthly*

*The Atlantic Monthly* is a highly respected magazine that features award-winning writing focusing on political issues, as well as humor pieces, fiction, and poetry. Art director Judy Garlan and her staff commission about twenty to thirty illustrations (mostly full color) for each issue. They work with established illustrators as well as newcomers, and they commission artists from all over the world.

"I'm always looking for the best. I like work that is sophisticated, elegant, and expertly executed. I'm not interested in imitators. I prefer to work with an artist who originates the style, rather than someone who's just adopting it," says Garlan.

She feels that illustrators should study the magazine before they send her their promotional pieces. "Just seeing pages from *The Atlantic* in illustration or design annuals is not enough. You really need to look through the magazine and read the articles to get a sense of the overall tone and the subject matters that the magazine deals with," she explains.

Illustrators should do their research in the library or at the local newsstand, and not call busy art directors for basic information. "It's very annoying to get calls from illustrators who know nothing about the magazine. They always end up keeping me on the phone for twenty minutes, asking things like, 'Who's the art director?,' ' How do you spell your name?,' 'What's your address?,' 'What kind of work are you looking for?'"

Garlan says she commissions many different styles of illustration. "I look for artists who have an obsession with a mood, a style, or a subject matter—artists who are on the edge of fine art. The best art—the pieces with the most creative energy, although inspired by the article and often discussed and sketched endlessly—is still first and foremost the artist's personal expression. Realism is fine, but it must have more spark than one gets from merely copying a photograph. It should be no less of a personal statement than highly stylized art," she says.

Pieces she can't use are one-liner cartoons and "melodramatic finger-pointing, political" illustrations. "Our text presents strong and controversial ideas in the belief that this allows readers to take in new information more easily, in an objective fashion," she states. "I don't want to put in an illustration where the reader will immediately think, 'Oh, I get it. This article is against George Bush. I don't need to read it.'" For Garlan, the pages work best when the art and the writing work like "two people on the same wavelength having an intelligent and lively conversation."

As for the fiction department, Garlan likes illustrations that set a scene and echo the tone of the story, that have a sense of narrative but convey a slight feeling of mystery by showing just a glimpse or a moment.

Like most magazines, *The Atlantic*'s fees for art are not set in stone. Price varies from project to project. However, the typical price for a cover is two thousand dollars; one thousand dollars for a full-page inside illustration, and several hundred dollars for spot illustrations, depending upon the size and number of the spots.

You can call Garlan for a drop-off appointment to review your portfolio. She looks through everything that comes in the mail and will return your work if you enclose a self-addressed, stamped envelope.

Judy Garlan
Art Director
*The Atlantic Monthly*
745 Boylston Street
Boston MA 02116
(617) 536-9500

Illustrator Theo Rudnak of Atlanta, Georgia, illustrated this cover for the February issue.

## DWAYNE FLINCHUM
## *OMNI*

*OMNI* Magazine does not commission illustrations. It purchases existing art from illustrators and fine artists. Most of the articles in *OMNI* involve scientific subjects such as space travel and futuristic automobile design. Art director Dwayne Flinchum searches for art that matches the article.

*OMNI* uses a picture file, gathered from research, and artists' submissions to locate appropriate pieces. Flinchum also looks through magazines, illustration annuals, and creative directories for appropriate images. "If we pick up art from a magazine, we try to pick it up from a magazine that's not widely read in this country," he explains.

If your style is surrealistic, fantasy or New Age, you can send a set of slides to Flinchum, and he'll put your work on a computer file. The *OMNI* art staff will contact you if they want to buy your illustration. Flinchum prefers to see high-quality surrealistic illustrations and oil paintings rather than the more typical science fiction "cartoony" styles. *OMNI* has bought published work from Brad Holland, Heather Cooper, and Rudolph Hausner, among others.

The pay rate is four hundred dollars for a single page, eight hundred dollars for an opening feature spread, and eight hundred dollars for a magazine cover.

Dwayne Flinchum
Art Director
*OMNI* Magazine
1965 Broadway
New York NY 10023
(212) 496-6100

Gottfried Helnwein's super-realistic style illustrated the fictional story, "Unidentified Objects."

## CHRIS CURRY
### *The New Yorker*

Chris Curry, illustration editor for *The New Yorker*, buys spot drawings for the events section of the magazine. She buys eight to twelve illustrations a week. "I look for artists who can do portraits of celebrities, but the illustrations should capture the spirit of the event we're promoting," Curry says. Most spot illustrations are reproduced in black and white.

Because *The New Yorker* is considered one of the best written magazines in the country, Curry has no trouble finding established illustrators and even fa-

mous contemporary painters to contribute spot illustrations. But Curry also welcomes contributions from talented new illustrators.

Wednesday is portfolio drop-off day. Just leave your book for Chris Curry at the receptionist's desk any Wednesday morning, or you can mail her samples of your work.

Chris Curry
Illustration Editor
*The New Yorker*
25 West 43rd Street
New York NY 10036
(212) 840-3800

---

28

MOVIE HOUSES—Cont'd

Jane Fonda, Gregory Peck, and Jimmy Smits.
Theatre 2: Through Oct. 12: "Uncle Buck" (John Hughes), with John Candy, Amy Madigan, Jean Kelly, Gaby Hoffman, and Macaulay Culkin. From Oct. 13: "Halloween 5: The Revenge of Michael Myers" (Dominique Othenin-Girard).

TIMES SQUARE AREA

CRITERION CENTER, B'way at 44th. (354-0900)
Theatre 1: "Batman" (†).
Theatre 2: "Johnny Handsome" (†).
Theatre 3: "Kickboxer" (directed by Mark DiSalle and David Worth), with Jean-Claude Van Damme.
Theatre 4: Through Oct. 12: "War Party" (Franc Roddam), with Billy Wirth and Kevin Dillon. From Oct. 13: "Look Who's Talking" (Amy Heckerling), with John Travolta and Kirstie Alley.
Theatre 5: "Lock Up" (John Flynn), with Sylvester Stallone, Donald Sutherland, John Amos, Darlanne Fluegel, and Sonny Landham.
Theatre 6: "Blood Fist."
EMBASSY 1, B'way at 46th. (302-0494)
"An Innocent Man" (Peter Yates), with Tom Selleck and F. Murray Abraham.
EMBASSY 2, 3, AND 4, 7th Ave. at 47th. (730-7262)
Theatre 2: "Indiana Jones and the Last Crusade" (†); and "Star Trek V: The Final Frontier" (William Shatner), with Shatner and Leonard Nimoy.
Theatre 3: Through Oct. 12: "Turner & Hooch" (Roger Spottiswoode), with Tom Hanks; and "Honey, I Shrunk the Kids" (†). From Oct. 13: "Savage Beach."
Theatre 4: "The Package" (Andrew Davis), with Gene Hackman, Joanna Cassidy, Tommy Lee Jones, and John Heard.
LOEWS ASTOR PLAZA, 44th St. at B'way. (869-8340)
"Black Rain" (Ridley Scott), with Michael Douglas, Andy Garcia, Ken Takakura, and Kate Capshaw.
NATIONAL TWIN, B'way at 44th. (869-0950)
Theatre 1: Through Oct. 12: "Old Gringo" (Luis Puenzo), with Jane Fonda, Gregory Peck, and Jimmy Smits. From Oct. 13: "The Fabulous Baker Boys" (†).
Theatre 2: From Oct. 13: "Parenthood" (†). From Oct. 13: "Halloween 5: The Revenge of Michael Myers" (Dominique Othenin-Girard).
WARNER, 7th Ave. between 42nd and 43rd. (764-6760)
Through Oct. 12: "Welcome Home" (Franklin J. Schaffner), with Kris Kristofferson, JoBeth Williams, Sam Waterston, and Brian Keith.

*Marlene Dietrich*

*James Stewart brought a drawling ease and sociability to the role of the strong, loquacious Western hero in "Destry Rides Again" (1939). Stewart's Destry—a lean, gentle lawman who won't use a gun until he's pushed to extremes—is also a talespinner who rarely trips over his own yarns. His rationality and backbone drive hard guys crazy. Set in a tough spot named Bottleneck, this superb, bare-knuckled comedy mixes brawling action and moral fables with slapstick, verbal wit, and sex appeal. Mar-*

From Oct. 18: "The Bridge on the River Kwai" (†).
CINEMA VILLAGE, 22 E. 12th. (924-3363)
Through Oct. 10: "Imagine" (1988, Andrew Solt), a documentary; and "Yellow Submarine" (1968, George Dunning), a full-length animated cartoon of the Beatles.
Oct. 11-12: "Virgin Machine" (1989, Monika Treut; in German), with Ina Blum; and "She Must Be Seeing Things" (1988, Sheila McLaughlin), with Sheila Dabney.
Oct. 13-14: "40 Deuce" (1985, Paul Morrissey), with Kevin Bacon and Orson Bean; and "Midnight Cowboy" (1969, John Schlesinger), with Dustin Hoffman, Jon Voight, Sylvia Miles, and Brenda Vaccaro.
Oct. 15: "Jules and Jim" (1962, François Truffaut; in French), with Jeanne Moreau, Oskar Werner, and Henri Serre; and "The 400 Blows" (1959, Truffaut; in French), with Jean-Pierre Léaud.
Oct. 16-17: "9½ Weeks" (1986, Adrian Lyne), with Mickey Rourke and Kim Basinger; and "Fatal Attraction" (†).
From Oct. 18: "Sammy and Rosie Get Laid" (†) and "Maurice" (†).
THALIA SOHO, 15 Vandam St. (675-0498)
Through Oct. 10: "The Reckless Moment" (1949, Max Ophuls), with James Mason and Joan Bennett; "Fallen Angel" (1945, Otto Preminger), with Alice Faye, Dana Andrews, and Linda Darnell; and "Each Dawn I Die" (1939, William Keighley), with James Cagney and George Raft.
Oct. 11-12: "Unfaithfully Yours" (1948, Preston Sturges), with Rex Harrison, Linda Darnell, and Barbara Lawrence; and "A Letter to Three Wives" (1949, Joseph L. Mankiewicz), with Linda Darnell, Jeanne Crain, Ann Sothern, Kirk Douglas, and Paul Douglas.
Oct. 13-14: "My Beautiful Laundrette" (1986, Stephen Frears), with Roshan Seth, Saeed Jaffrey, Gordon Warnecke, and Daniel Day Lewis; and "Gumshoe" (1972, Frears), with Albert Finney.
Oct. 15: "The Adversary" (1971, Satyajit Ray), with Dhritiman Chatterjee; and "Mahanagar" (†).
Oct. 16-17: "The Big Combo" (1955, Joseph H. Lewis), with Cornell Wilde, Jean Wallace, Richard Conte, and Brian Donlevy; "Deadline—U.S.A." (1952, Richard Brooks), with Humphrey Bogart, Kim Hunter, and Ethel Barrymore; and "He Walked by Night" (1949, Alfred Werker), with Richard Basehart and Scott Brady.
From Oct. 18: "Broadcast News" (1987, James L. Brooks), with William Hurt, Albert Brooks, Holly Hunter, Joan Cusack, Lois Chiles, Robert Prosky, and Jack Nicholson; and "Real Life" (1979, Albert Brooks), with Brooks and Charles Grodin.

Caricature by New Yorker Robert de Michiell of Marlene Dietrich for *The New Yorker's* "Top of the Town" section.

## GARY SLUZEWSKI
### *Cleveland Magazine*

Art director Gary Sluzewski hires illustrators from all over the country. "With Federal Express and the fax machine I don't have to reiy on local talent." However, Sluzewski will see any artist who wants to show him his portfolio. "It's a small market, so I have the time to see everybody. Don't just pop in. Call and make an appointment," he advises.

He looks for illustrations that are conceptual and expressive. "I'm seeing a lot of portfolios with work geared toward the advertising market. These illustrations look like they were done by committee. For the editorial market, you need to show work with a personal vision," he says.

Sluzewski welcomes mail promotions. "I keep almost everything on file, because I'll never know when I need a particular style."

*Cleveland Magazine* pays seventy-five dollars and up for spot illustrations, and four hundred dollars for a full-page illustration.

Gary Sluzewski
Art Director
*Cleveland Magazine*
1621 Euclid Avenue
Cleveland OH 44115
(216) 771-2833

© Karen Stolper. Used with permission.

Karen Stolper of New York City created this illustration for an article on what to do when you are snowbound in Cleveland.

*Far too many infants in Cleveland die before
their first birthdays. Most of them are black.
Politics is partly to blame.*

# THE SILENT Cry

An electric fan blows warm, stale air through the living room of the decaying frame house on East 59th Street where the Hendersons live. Sabrina Henderson cradles her infant daughter, Nakii, as she sits on a sagging couch. Sabrina's twin, Saprina, tries to stretch out comfortably on the floor, though her swollen belly makes that difficult. Saprina is expecting in November.

Seven-month-old Nakii's curly black hair is speckled with blue-and-white plastic butterfly barrettes, and she stretches her tiny hand as she naps on her 15-year-old mother's lap. Sabrina coos and laughs with pleasure at holding the beautiful baby that belongs to her, smiling at her as if she were one of the dolls she played with a few years ago instead of a hungry, demanding and needy child. Nakii's bottle, filled with Faygo root beer, rests precariously on the sticky coffee table.

Nakii is lucky. Protected in her mother's lap, she is still young enough to be oblivious to the danger around her. Weeks ago, a sweltering night was punctuated by the crash of bricks hitting the house. One brick was heaved at the window next to Nakii's crib, impeded only by a flimsy chicken-wire screen.

78 CLEVELAND • OCTOBER 1988

ILLUSTRATION•DAN REED

BY
EVELYN
THEISS

Illustrator Dan Reed of
Providence, Rhode Island,
created this somber illustration
for an article on infant mortality
in the city.

## D.J. STOUT
*Texas Monthly*

*Texas Monthly* is a beautifully art directed magazine with a tradition of publishing great illustrations. "I commission a lot of creative portraits, so I'm always looking for artists who can capture the likeness and the personality of the subject," says art director D.J. Stout. Most of the illustrations are done by established illustrators from around the country. "One way to break in is to do spot illustrations for the magazine. If I see good concepts in the spot illustrations, I may ask for a full page or even a cover."

Although Stout sets aside a few days a month to review portfolios, he prefers that you just send him promotional pieces. "I'm very understaffed, so I don't have time to see everybody. You can send in your portfolio by mail, but please enclose a self-addressed, stamped envelope or give me your Federal Express number." If you want to show Stout your portfolio in person, call him for an appointment.

*Texas Monthly* pays one thousand dollars for the cover, eight hundred to one thousand dollars for full-page illustrations, and two hundred to four hundred dollars for spot illustrations.

D.J. Stout
*Texas Monthly*
Art Director
P.O. Box 1569
Austin TX 78767
(512) 476-7085

Illustrator Theo Rudnak's use of deep red and smoke emerging from a chile's mouth depict the hotness of the only chile that is native to Texas.

Illustration by Stephen Alcorn
of Cambridge, New York, for
the article, "Amigo," which
notes one man's thoughts on
the nature of friendship.

## JUDI RADICE
### *Spectrum Foods, INC.*

As Design and Marketing Director of San Francisco's Spectrum Foods, Inc., Judi Radice hires designers and illustrators to create menus, match boxes, T-shirts, napkins, signage, take-out packages, and stationery for a chain of innovative upscale restaurants. The restaurants are located throughout the West coast, and each has a special theme and requires unique graphic treatment.

Radice prefers working with established design firms when doing large-scale projects, which might include signage and graphic applications for a complete line of restaurant ware, from menus to napkins and wine labels.

But for smaller projects, such as redesigning an existing menu or stationery, she likes to give talented young designers an opportunity to work with Spectrum Foods.

Because the artwork needs to be applicable to many different products, such as promotional T-shirts and packaging, Radice prefers to hire designers who have a thorough knowledge of production and are willing to challenge the limits. "I'm interested in what the final product looks like: if you can be creative on the production end, you can make a job look great even if it only uses two colors," Radice explains.

Radice reviews portfolios and welcomes self-promotional materials from designers and illustrators.

Judi Radice
Design and Marketing Director
Spectrum Foods, Inc.
617 Front Street
San Francisco CA 94111
(415) 398-5704

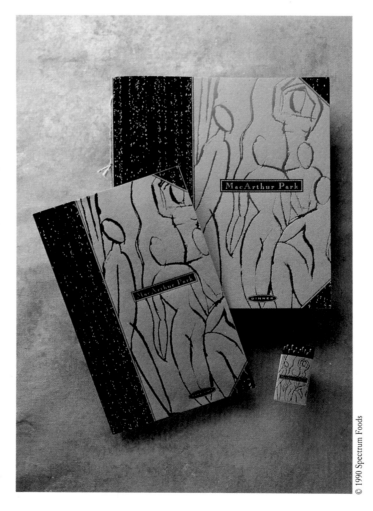

Freelancer Jennifer Morla of San Francisco created this menu design for Radice's client, MacArthur Park Restaurants.

© 1990 Spectrum Foods

# *Resources*

Not being a member of a corporate support group can leave you feeling out of touch and isolated. This makes it all the more important for you to find those organizations and activities that are designed to help freelancers cope with this fast-paced, competitive industry. Joining professional organizations, attending design conferences, and sending work to illustration and design competitions will help you stay current with marketing and stylistic trends. Here's a partial listing of professional organizations, trade publications, competitions, and advertising and promotional vehicles. You can write to the ones you're interested in for more information.

## ORGANIZATIONS OF INTEREST

### Advertising Club of Greater St. Louis
*400 Mansion House Center*
*St. Louis MO 63102*
Established in 1901 as the St. Louis charter of the American Advertising Federation, the Institute of Advertising is an annual venture with major St. Louis graduate schools covering all aspects of advertising and marketing trends.

### Advertising Club of Kansas City
*1 Ward Parkway Center #102*
*Kansas City MO 64112*
Serves as a forum to promote a better understanding of the advertising, marketing, and communications industry and its values. Offers workshops and seminars.

### Advertising Club of Los Angeles
*3600 Wilshire Boulevard #432*
*Los Angeles CA 90010*
*(213) 382-1228*
Los Angeles chapter serves as a forum to promote the communications industry. (See Advertising Club of New York.)

### Advertising Club of New York
*155 East 55th Street #202*
*New York NY 10022*
*(212) 935-8080*
Established in 1906 to foster understanding and knowledge of advertising, marketing, and related fields. Offers courses in advertising and marketing. Annual Addy Awards for creative excellence.

### American Center for Design
*233 East Ontario #500*
*Chicago IL 60611*
*(312) 787-2018*
National organization which represents all industry segments through a national network of advertising professionals, educators, and students. Also serves as a national center for information regarding the role and value of design. Known as the Society of Typographic Arts when it was founded in 1927, ACD hosts a Creativity Conference, design management seminars, speaker programs, and a design student conference.

### American Council for the Arts
*1285 Avenue of the Americas, 3rd Floor*
*New York NY 10019*
*(212) 245-4510*
Fosters government support of the arts. Lobbies in favor of artists' rights. Publishes monthly newsletter and offers discounts from ACA books.

### American Institute of Graphic Arts (AIGA)
*1059 3rd Avenue*
*New York NY 10021*
*(212) 752-0813*
Founded in 1914, this is one of the most prestigious design organizations in the country. It fosters knowledge about graphic design and upholds ethical standards of the industry. Offers lectures, seminars, a biannual conference, and a computerized membership list. Publishes quarterly newsletter and awards annual.

**American Society of Magazine Photographers (ASMP)**
205 Lexington Avenue
New York NY 10016
(212) 889-9144
Founded in 1944, ASMP is a professional society that works to evolve good trade practices for the photographer in the communications field. Presents awards, maintains a reference library, sponsors educational programs and seminars. Publishes monthly newsletter.

**Art Action**
Canadian Artists Representation
36 8th Street
Ottawa, Ontario K1P 5K5 Canada
(613) 235-6277
Founded in 1968, this nonprofit organization lobbies for artists' rights. Publishes updates on health hazards, copyright, and moral rights legislation. Provides standard contracts used in the industry.

**Art Directors and Artists Club of Sacramento**
2791 24th Street
Sacramento CA 95818
(916) 731-8802
Promotes best possible opportunities for professional development and instruction. Sponsors Envision and Business by Design conferences. Offers scholarships and portfolio reviews.

**Art Directors Club Inc.**
250 Park Avenue South
New York NY 10003
(212) 674-0500
Trade organization founded in 1920 for graphic arts professionals. Members include art directors of agencies, magazines, and designers; associate members are artists, photographers, copywriters, and cinematographers.

**Art Directors Club of Los Angeles**
7080 Hollywood Boulevard #410
Los Angeles CA 90028
(213) 465-8707
(213) 465-1787
Founded in 1948 to foster communication between art directors and others in the communications field. Sponsors monthly lectures and The Best in the West Awards.

**Artist's Equity**
P.O. Box 28068
Central Station
Washington DC 20038
(202) 628-9633
Nonprofit organization established as a nonpolitical group to advance the cultural, legislative, professional, and economic interests of visual artists, such as painters, sculptors, and printmakers.

**Association of Medical Illustrators**
2692 Huguenot Springs Road
Midlothian VA 23113
(804) 794-2908
International nonprofit organization for illustrators specializing in medical illustration. Offers job hotline, membership directory, mailing service, discounted prices for all publications, workshops, regional and annual meetings.

**Association of Professional Design Firms**
685 High Street #5
Worthington OH 43085
(614) 888-3301
Fax: 1 (614) 888-3373
Organization of design firms that promotes the value and awareness of design and the design consultant to various business and educational audiences. Holds an annual meeting.

**Business/Professional Advertising Association**
100 Metroplex Drive #401
Edison NJ 08817
Association for business-to-business communications professionals. Offers workshops, meetings, seminars, newsletters, handbooks, and conferences.

**Cartoonists Guild**
c/o Graphic Artists Guild
11 West 20th Street
New York NY 10011
(212) 463-7730
Founded in 1967, this is a division of the Graphic Artists Guild. It consists of cartoonists working for magazines, syndicates, book publishers, TV, and advertising. Its purpose is to raise the business and ethical standards of the industry and to provide legal and educational services to members.

### The Center for Computer Graphics for Design
*45 Stephenson Terrace*
*Briarcliff Manor NY 10510*
*(914) 741-2850*
Brings computer graphics to the visual design community and protects and nurtures design's role in using that technology. Sponsors two conferences a year: The New Designer (June) and The New Technology (December).

### The Children's Book Council
*67 Irving Place*
*New York NY 10276*
*(212) 254-2666*
Members are publishers of children's books interested in promoting literature for children. Sponsors the Children's Book Week each November.

### Color Marketing Group
*4001 North 9th Street #102*
*Arlington VA 22203*
*(703) 528-7666*
*(703) 522-1853*
Since 1962, the Color Marketing Group has been committed to color as the ultimate marketing tool and a belief that sharing noncompetitive information can reap positive rewards. Offers information on color marketing, trends, styling, and design. National and regional meetings, workshops, and forums. Issues Color Directions (color chips that reflect currently popular colors).

### Dallas Society of Visual Communicators
*3530 High Mesa Drive*
*Dallas TX 75234*
*(214) 241-2017*
Founded in 1957, its members include art directors, designers, illustrators, photographers, writers, and production artists. Offers monthly meetings, scholarships and an intern program. Holds the annual Dallas Show, which covers an eight state area.

### Design Management Institute
*777 Boylston Street*
*Boston MA 02116-2603*
*(617) 236-4165*
*Fax: 1 (617) 424-8740*
Founded in 1976, it shares management techniques as applies to design groups and facilitates better understanding of the role design can play in achieving business goals. Sponsors five conferences a year, including the annual conference at Martha's Vineyard. Holds seminars for design professionals. Publishes *Design Management Journal.*

### Graphic Artists Guild
*11 West 20th Street*
*New York NY 10011*
*(212) 463-7730*
National resource and advocacy organization. Formulates ethical guidelines, sponsors workshops, lobbies for artists' rights. Offers artist representation and negotiation, discounts on art supplies, an accounting referral service, and group insurance. Publishes a pricing guide.

### Graphic Artists Guild
*P.O. Box 1454 GMF*
*Boston MA 02205*
*(617) 451-5362*
The Boston chapter is one of the most active in the country. Offers seminars, annual Boston See Party (portfolio review), workshops, and courses.

### Greeting Card Association
*1350 New York Avenue Northwest #615*
*Washington DC 20005*
*(202) 393-1778*
Founded in 1941, the GCA is composed of publishers of greeting cards and suppliers of materials. Publishes a monthly newsletter, annual Artists and Writers Market List, and the annual Greeting Card Industry Directory. GCA created the Greeting Card Creative Network to help build a network of strong working relationships between creators, publishers and suppliers.

### Guild of Natural Science Illustrators, Inc.
*Box 652 Ben Franklin Station*
*Washington DC 20044*
*(202) 357-2128*
Nonprofit organization of artists who earn their living wholly or in part through the production of scientific illustration. Founded in 1969, this organization offers workshops, monthly and annual meetings, a newsletter, and member exhibits.

### Industrial Designers Society of America
*1142 East Walker Road*
*Great Falls VA 22066*
*(703) 759-0100*
Maintains professional standards for business, industry, government, and international designers.

**Institute of Business Designers**
*341 Merchandise Mart*
*Chicago IL 60654*
*(312) 467-1950*
Represents contract interior design professionals who specialize in commercial and institutional design. Offers educational programs, national conference, bimonthly national newsletter, legislative bulletin, and forms and documents manual.

**International Society of Copier Artists**
*800 West End Avenue*
*New York NY 10025*
*(212) 662-5533*
Society composed of artists exploring the artistic uses of photocopiers.

**National Cartoonists Society**
*9 Ebony Court*
*Brooklyn NY 11229*
Founded in 1946, this is a professional society of cartoonists; associate members are editors, writers, and those interested in the craft.

**National Computer Graphics Association**
*2722 Merrilee Drive #200*
*Fairfax VA 22031*
*(703) 698-9600*
*(800) 225-NCGA*
Founded in 1979, the NCGA is composed of people and organizations who use, manufacture, and sell computer graphics hardware and software. Operates computer graphics resource center, sponsors competitions, bestows awards, and conducts seminars. Publishes monthly newsletter.

**The One Club**
*3 West 18th Street*
*New York NY 10011*
*(212) 255-7070*
Promotes excellence in advertising, copywriting, and design. Sponsors The One Show. Features portfolio reviews and an annual lecture series.

**Pantone Color Institute**
*6324 Varill Avenue #319*
*Woodland Hills CA 91367*
*(818) 340-2370*
Twenty-five years ago Pantone launched the Pantone Matching System, a comprehensive color communication system. In 1985, the company established the nonprofit Pantone Color Institute to study color trends, the psychology of color, and other color-related topics. Its free quarterly newsletter features results of the latest color studies and articles on color-related topics.

**Phoenix Society of Communicating Arts**
*P.O. Box 1346*
*Phoenix AZ 85001*
*(602) 381-0304*
Nonprofit organization made up of professionals in graphic design and advertising. Members include art directors, designers, writers, illustrators, photographers, and students. Its purpose is to promote the interests of the communicating arts in Phoenix and throughout Arizona. It sponsors monthly programs with well-known speakers and the biannual On the Edge Symposium. Publishes the PRISMA Awards Showbook featuring award winners in the society's annual competition.

**Sacramento Regional Illustrators' Guild**
*P.O. Box 161382*
*Sacramento CA 95814*
*(916) 685-4147*
Association composed primarily of northern California illustrators and artists. Founded in 1962, its purpose is to promote and stimulate interest in the continued use of illustration and to aid illustrators in business matters, ethics, referrals, and promotion. Members sponsor exhibits, an annual show, and speakers' programs, and contribute time to numerous organizations.

**San Francisco Art Director's Club**
*2757 16th Street Box 277*
*San Francisco CA 94103*
*(415) 387-4040*
Organization of creative advertising and design professionals in the Bay Area.

**Seattle Design Association**
*P.O. Box 1097*
*Main Office Station*
*Seattle WA 98111*
Members are graphic, industrial and textile designers, illustrators and photographers, art directors, production artists, and reps. Sponsors biannual juried competition, biannual art auction. Monthly meetings feature noted speakers. Publishes monthly newsletter. Job Bank provides designers with job leads.

### Society of Children's Book Writers
P.O. Box 296
Mar Vista Station
Los Angeles CA 90066
(818) 347-2849
Founded in 1968, this organization acts as a network for the exchange of knowledge among children's writers, editors, publishers, illustrators, and agents. Annual conference features portfolio review. Publishes bimonthly newsletter.

### Society of Environmental Graphic Designers
47 3rd Street
Cambridge MA 02141
Founded in 1978, this nonprofit professional organization represents those involved in signage. It suggests standards and guidelines for the profession. National conference is held annually. Publishes sourcebooks for materials and manufacturers.

### Society of Illustrators
128 East 63rd Street
New York NY 10021
(212) 838-2560
Created in 1901 to promote interest in the art of illustration. Has annual juried show and student scholarship exhibition.

### Society of Illustrators of Los Angeles
5000 Van Nuys #400
Sherman Oaks CA 91403
(818) 784-0588
Organizations of professional illustrators with members throughout the Western states. Speaker program, pricing sessions, nonjuried membership art show, and scholarships. Hosts Illustration West, a juried exhibition of original illustration.

### Society of Newspaper Design
c/o The Newspaper Center
P.O. Box 17290
Dulles International Airport
Washington DC 20041
(703) 620-1083
Members include reporters, editors, publishers, artists, photographers, and designers employed in newspapers or related businesses. Holds regional seminars and workshops. Sponsors annual design competition. Publishes bimonthly journal.

### Society of Photographers & Artists Representatives (SPAR)
1123 Broadway #914
New York NY 10010
(212) 924-6023
Professional nationwide organization of representatives for photography and illustration. Offers general meetings, special seminars, newsletters, and special bulletins. Special services include portfolio reviews, mailing labels, membership directory, and a rep kit (set of business forms).

### Society of Publications Designers
603 42nd Street #1416
New York NY 10165
(212) 983-8585
Founded in 1964, this organization includes art directors, designers, editors, and graphic artists who lay out and design consumer, business, and professional publications and newspapers. Sponsors annual design competition. Has speakers' bureau.

### Type Directors Club
60 East 42nd Street #1130
New York NY 10165-0015
(212) 983-6042
Professional society of typographic designers, type directors, and teachers of typography. Holds international typography competition, seminars, and monthly luncheon lectures. Publishes a magazine three times a year.

### University and College Designers Association
2811 Mishawaka Avenue
South Bend IN 46615
(219) 288-UCDA
Created to improve the stature and credibility of designers and art directors within the academic community. Sponsors annual conference, seminars, and workshops.

### Visual Artists & Galleries Association, Inc.
1 Rockefeller Plaza #2626
New York NY 10020
(212) 397-8353
Fax: 1(212) 974-0748
Has been working for artists' rights and copyright since 1978. Keeps members updated on copyright law. Will collect royalty fees on members' behalf. Initial legal advice and referral sources for all problems in the field of visual arts. Acts as an agent for artists in negotiating licenses. Publishes a quarterly newsletter.

*Volunteer Lawyers for the Arts*
*1285 Avenue of the Americas, 3rd Floor*
*New York NY 10019*
*(212) 977-9270*
VLA was founded in 1969 to provide the arts community with free legal assistance and comprehensive legal education. Artists and arts organizations that cannot afford private counsel are eligible for VLA's legal services for arts-related legal problems.

*Western Art Directors Club*
*P.O. Box 996*
*Palo Alto CA 94302*
Founded in 1965, WADC stimulates communication among those involved in the communicating arts. Members include art directors, designers, marketing communications professionals, writers, illustrators, photographers, teachers, typographers, and students. Sponsors annual West Coast Show.

*Women in Design*
*400 West Madison #2400*
*Chicago IL 60606*
*(312) 648-1874*
Nonprofit professional organization that focuses on the goals and interests of designers. Members include both men and women employed in design, illustration, and photography. Offers seminars, discussion groups, and exhibits. Bimonthly newsletters and a membership directory are published.

## CONFERENCES AND SEMINARS

*ACM Siggraph*
*Conference Management*
*111 East Wacker Drive #600*
*Chicago IL 60610*
*(312) 644-6610*
*(212) 752-0911*
Conference on computer design.

*AIGA Minnesota Design Conference*
*AIGA*
*International Market Square*
*275 Market Street #54*
*Minneapolis MN 55405*
*(612) 332-3993*

*AIGA National Conference*
*1059 Third Avenue*
*New York NY 10021*
*(212) 752-0813*

*Art Supply Expo*
*(formerly Tools of the Trade)*
*1516 South Pontius Avenue*
*Los Angeles CA 90025*
*(213) 477-8521*

*Computer Graphics Show*
*817 Silversprings Avenue #409*
*Silversprings MD 20904*
*(301) 587-4545*

*Creativity Conference*
*American Center for Design*
*233 East Ontario #500*
*Chicago IL 60611*
*(312) 787-2018*
*Fax: 1(312) 649-9518*
Biannual conference of presentations and workshops on creativity.

*The Design Conference That Just Happens to Be in Park City*
*P.O. Box 726*
*Park City UT 84060*
*(213) 557-2773*

*The Design Management Institute*
*777 Boylston Street*
*Boston MA 02116-2603*
*(617) 236-1315*
Annual conference at Martha's Vineyard.

*Desktop Presentation Graphics Conference & Exposition*
*Cambridge Marketing, Inc.*
*1 Forbes Road*
*Lexington MA 02173*
*(617) 860-7100*

*Dynamic Graphics Educational Foundation*
*P.O. Box 1901*
*6000 North Forest Park Drive*
*Peoria IL 61614-3592*
*(309) 688-8866*
Workshops in production, design, and electronic design.

*Envision*
*Art Directors and Artists Club*
*2791 24th Street*
*Sacramento CA 95818*
*(916) 731-8802*
Conference on design trends.

*Folio Show*
*Folio Publishing Corp.*
*P.O. Box 4949*
*6 River Bend*
*Stamford CT 06907-0949*
*(203) 358-9900*
Production, editing, and marketing of magazines.

*Grafix*
*Conference Management Corp.*
*200 Connecticut Avenue*
*Norwalk CT 06856-4990*
*(203) 852-0500*
Computer design conference.

*Graphic Communication*
*Edgell Expositions*
*747 3rd Avenue*
*New York NY 10017*
*(212) 418-4118*

*Illustrators' Conference*
*Society of Children's Book Writers*
*P.O. Box 296*
*MarVista Station*
*Los Angeles CA 90066*
*(818) 347-2849*
Seminars on the children's book industry plus a portfolio review.

*Industrial Designers Society of America*
*1142 East Walker Road*
*Great Falls VA 22066*
*(703) 759-0100*
National conference.

*Influences*
*Marshall University*
*Huntington WV 25701*
*(212) 486-5259*
Trends in design and photography.

*International Color Marketing Conference*
*Color Marketing Group*
*4001 North 9th Street #102*
*Arlington VA 22203*
*(703) 528-7666*
Explores the impact color has on interior design, graphic design, fashion, and lifestyles. Previews palette forecasts.

*International Design Conference in Aspen*
*P.O. Box 664*
*Aspen CO 81612*
*(303) 925-2257*

*Magazine Publishing Week*
*911 Hope Street*
*P.O. Box 4949*
*6 River Bend Center*
*Stamford CT 06907-0949*
*(203) 358-9900, ext. 395*
*Fax: 1(203) 358-0594*
Seminars on magazine publishing trends.

*The New Designer*
*Center for Computer for Design*
*45 Stephenson Terrace*
*Briarcliff Manor NY 10510*
*(914) 741-2850*
How the computer affects the designer.

*The New Tools*
*Center for Computer for Design*
*45 Stephenson Terrace*
*Briarcliff Manor NY 10510*
*(914) 741-2850*
Technological trends in computers.

*On the Edge Symposium*
*Phoenix Society of Communicating Arts*
*P.O. Box 1346*
*Phoenix AZ 85001*
*(602) 266-1301*
Retreat at the Grand Canyon to discuss design.

*Seybold Seminars*
*P.O. Box 578*
*6922 Wildlife Road*
*Malibu CA 90265-0578*
*(213) 457-5850*
*Fax: 1(213) 457-4704*
Seminars on computer publishing.

*Stanford Publishing Course*
*Stanford Alumni Association*
*Bowman Alumni House*
*Stanford CA 94304*
*(415) 725-1083*
Annual two-week course on magazine and book publishing.

*Type Conference*
*Type Directors Club*
*545 West 45th Street*
*New York NY 10036*
*(212) 983-6042*

*University and College Designers Association*
*2811 Mishawaka Avenue*
*South Bend IN 46615*
*(219) 288-UCDA*
Seminars on how design trends affect the nonprofit designer.

# Major Award Annuals

*ADLA Annual*
*Art Directors Club of Los Angeles*
*1258 North Highland #209*
*Los Angeles CA 90038*
*(213) 465-8707*
Circulation: 6,000
Entry fee: $15
Entry deadline: July

*American Illustration*
*49 East 21st Street*
*New York NY 10010*
*(212) 979-4500*
Circulation: 10,000
Entry fee: $17
Entry deadline: March

*Annual of American Illustration*
*Society of Illustrators*
*128 East 63rd Street*
*New York NY 10021*
*(212) 838-2560*
Circulation: 10,000
Entry fee: $15
Entry deadline: October

*Art Directors Annual*
*Art Directors Club*
*250 Park Avenue South*
*New York NY 10003*
*(212) 674-0500*
Circulation: 20,000
Entry fee: $20
Entry deadline: May

*The Book Show*
*AIGA*
*1059 3rd Avenue*
*New York NY 10021*
*(212) 752-0813*
Circulation: 12,000
Entry fee: $18
Entry deadline: December

*CA Design Annual*
*CA Illustration Annual*
*Communication Arts*
*P.O. Box 10300*
*410 Sherman Avenue*
*Palo Alto CA 94303*
Circulation: 60,000
Entry fee: $15 (design); $12 (illustration)
Entry deadline: July (design); March (illustration)

*Communication Graphics*
*AIGA*
*1059 3rd Avenue*
*New York NY 10021*
*(212) 752-0813*
Circulation: 12,000
Entry fee: $18
Entry deadline: February

*Creativity*
*Art Direction Magazine*
*10 East 39th Street*
*New York NY 10016*
*(212) 889-6500*
Circulation: 10,000
Entry fee: $14 for a single entry; $28 for campaign
Entry deadline: May

*DESI Graphics Awards*
*Graphic Design: USA*
*32 Gansevoort*
*New York NY 10014*

(212) 741-7331
Circulation: 2,000
Entry fee: $12
Entry deadline: February

**Graphis International Yearbooks**
(Design, Annual Reports, Posters, Photos)
Graphis
107 Dufourstrasse
CH-8008 Zurich
Switzerland
Circulation: 12,000
Entry fee: $10 single entry; $25 campaign entry
Entry deadline: January

**Mead Annual Report Show**
Mead Paper
Courthouse Plaza Northeast
Dayton OH 45463
(513) 222-6323
Circulation: 15,000
Entry fee: $15
Entry deadline: May

**100 Show Annual**
American Center for Design
233 East Ontario #500
Chicago IL 60611
(312) 787-2018
Fax: 1(312) 649-9518
Circulation: 6,000
Entry fee: For members $20 for single entry, $30 for
campaign entry; for nonmembers $25 for single entry, $35
for campaign entry
Entry deadline: November

**The One Show**
The One Club
3 West 18th Street
New York NY 10011
(212) 255-7070
Circulation: 8,500
Entry fee: $45
Entry deadline: June

**Print Casebooks**
104 5th Avenue
New York NY 10011
(212) 463-0600
Circulation: 7,500

Entry fee: $10-25
Entry deadline: June

**Print Regional Design Annual**
104 5th Avenue, 9th Floor
New York NY 10011
(212) 463-0600
Circulation: 62,000
Entry fee: $12.50
Entry deadline: March

**Publication Design Annual**
Society of Publications Designers
603 42nd Street #1416
New York NY 10165
(212) 983-8585
Entry fee: $20 for members for single entry; $30 for
nonmembers.

## RECOMMENDED PUBLICATIONS

**Advertising Age**
220 East 42nd Street.
New York NY 10017
(212) 210-0100
Weekly advertising and marketing tabloid.

**Adweek**
A/S/M/ Communications, Inc.
49 East 21st Street
New York NY 10010
(212) 529-5500
Weekly advertising and marketing magazine.

**Airbrush Action**
317 Cross Street
Lakewood NJ 08701
(201) 364-2111
Bimonthly magazine featuring product news and trends
in airbrushing.

**Archive**
American Showcase
724 5th Avenue
New York NY 10019-4182
(212) 245-0981
Bimonthly magazine featuring outstanding international
ad campaigns.

*Artist's Market*
*F&W Publications*
*1507 Dana Avenue*
*Cincinnati OH 45207*
*(513) 531-2222*
Annual directory listing magazines, book publishers, greeting card companies, and other markets seeking freelance artwork.

*Audio Video Market Place*
*R.R. Bowker Co.*
*245 West 17th Street*
*New York NY 10011*
*(212) 645-9700*
Directory listing audiovisual and film companies.

*Chicago Midwest Flash*
*Alexander Communications*
*212 West Superior Street #400*
*Chicago IL 60610*
*(312) 944-5115*
Quarterly magazine featuring articles and news on graphic art and advertising in the Midwest.

*Communication Arts*
*P.O. Box 10300*
*410 Sherman Avenue*
*Palo Alto CA 94303*
*(415) 326-6040*
Magazine covering design, illustration, and photography. Published eight times a year.

*The Design Firm Directory*
*Wefler & Associates, Inc.*
*P.O. Box 1591*
*Evanston IL 60204*
*(312) 454-1940*
Annual directory listing design firms.

*Folio*
*P.O. Box 4949*
*Stamford CT 06907-0949*
*(203) 358-9900*
Monthly magazine featuring trends in magazine circulation, production, and editorial.

*Gale Directory of Publications*
*Gale Research Co.*
*Penobscot Building*
*Detroit MI 48226*

Annual guide to newspapers, magazines, and journals.

*Graphis*
*141 Lexington Avenue*
*New York NY 10017*
*(212) 682-0989*
Bimonthly international journal of graphic design.

*Handbook: Pricing & Ethical Guidelines*
*Graphic Artists Guild*
*F&W Publications*
*1507 Dana Avenue*
*Cincinnati OH 45207*
*(513) 531-2222*
Biannual guide to pricing illustration and design.

*HOW*
*F&W Publications*
*1507 Dana Avenue*
*Cincinnati OH 45207*
*(513) 531-2222*
Bimonthly magazine providing instruction on design methods for visual communicators on all levels.

*ID: Magazine of International Design*
*330 West 42nd Street*
*New York NY 10036*
*(212) 695-4955*
This bimonthly publication covers graphic, industrial, and packaging design.

*ITC Desktop*
*International Typeface Corp.*
*2 Hammarskjold Plaza*
*New York NY 10017*
*(212) 371-0699*
Bimonthly magazine aimed at desktop publishing for business communication.

*Macworld*
*501 2nd Street*
*San Francisco CA 94107*
*(415) 243-0505*
Monthly magazine written for the educated business Macintosh user. Includes product reviews and industry updates. Stresses solutions analysis, consumer issues, and trends in personal computing.

*O'Dwyer Directory of Public Relations Firms*
*J.R. O'Dwyer Co., Inc.*

271 Madison Avenue
New York NY 10016.
(212) 679-2471
Annual directory listing public relations firms, indexed by specialties.

## PC World
501 2nd Street
San Francisco CA 94107
(415) 243-0500
Solutions-oriented monthly reference magazine for business and professional users of IBM personal computers. It contains reviews, tutorials, and practical hands-on advice.

## Print
104 5th Avenue, 9th Floor
New York NY 10011
(212) 682-0830
Bimonthly magazine focusing on creative trends and technological advances in illustration, design, photography, and printing.

## Publish!
501 2nd Street
San Francisco CA 94107
(415) 243-0600
Monthly magazine devoted to desktop and personal computer publishing. Information ranges from laser printers and page make-up software to commercial typesetting systems that interface with personal computers.

## Publishers Weekly
205 West 42nd Street
New York NY 10017
(212) 463-6812
Weekly magazine covering industry trends and news in book publishing, book reviews, and interviews.

## Push!
Push Communications, Inc.
284 Fifth Ave.
New York NY 10001
(212) 268-4428
Quarterly magazine for art directors, designers and photographers.

## Select Magazine
153 West 18th Street

New York NY 10011
(212) 929-4473
Quarterly magazine distributed to ad agencies, photographers, production companies, and designers.

## Standard Directory of Advertising Agencies
National Register Publishing Co.
3004 Glenview Road
Wilmette IL 60901
(312) 256-6067
(800) 323-4601
Annual directory listing advertising agencies.

## Standard Periodical Directory
Oxbridge Communications, Inc.
Room 301, 150 5th Avenue
New York NY 10011
(212) 741-0231
Biannual directory listing magazines, journals, newsletters, directories, and association publications.

## Standard Rate and Data Service
3004 Glenview Road
Wilmette IL 60091
(312) 256-6067
(800) 323-4601
Annual directory listing magazines, plus their advertising rates.

## Step-by-Step Graphics
Dynamic Graphics
6000 North Forest Park Drive
Peoria IL 61614-3597
(309) 688-2300
Bimonthly magazine featuring instruction for graphic design and illustration projects.

## Studio
124 Galaxy
Rexdale, Ontario
M9W 4Y6
Canada
(416) 675-1999
Canada's leading design magazine features typography, illustration, and photography. Yearly competition is featured in the December issue. Published seven times a year (this includes the annual).

## Thomas Register of Manufacturers
Thomas Publishing Co.

1 Penn Plaza
New York NY 10001
(212) 695-0500
Multivolume directory listing manufacturers in all facets
of business.

*Ulrich's International Periodicals Directory*
R.R. Bowker Co.
245 West 17th Street
New York NY 10011
Annual directory listing international publications.

*Upper & Lower Case*
2 Hammarskjold Plaza
New York NY 10007
(212) 371-0699
Quarterly magazine featuring creative typography for
graphic artists and type directors.

*Working Press of the Nation*
National Research Bureau
310 South Michigan Avenue #1150
Chicago IL 60604
Annual directory listing book publishers, magazines, and
other markets that seek freelance writing.

*Writer's Market*
F&W Publications
1507 Dana Avenue
Cincinnati OH 45207
(513) 531-2222
(800) 289-0963
Annual directory listing book publishers, magazines, and
other publishing opportunities.

## CREATIVE DIRECTORIES

*American Showcase*
724 5th Avenue
New York NY 10019
(212) 245-0981
*Categories*: American Showcase offers one of the largest
directories. One volume lists illustrators, designers, and
reps; another volume lists photographers.
*Distribution*: Worldwide to 40,000 ad agencies, public
relations firms, publishing houses, record companies, TV
stations, government agencies, and corporations.
*Rates*: Full-page color $3,000; full-page b&w $2,500.
*Reprints*: 2,000 free.

*Arizona Portfolio*
815 North 1st Avenue #1
Phoenix AZ 85003
(602) 252-2332
*Categories*: Graphic design, illustration, photography,
calligraphy, and animation. Also lists reps and suppliers.
This is the only directory to focus exclusively on Arizona's
creative community.
*Distribution*: 10,000 in nine Southwestern states, 500 in
other major cities in the Midwest and East.
*Rates*: Full-page color $1,500.
*Reprints*: 500.

*Chicago Creative Directory*
333 North Michigan Avenue #810
Chicago IL 60601
(312) 236-7337
*Categories*: Illustration, design, photography, advertising
agencies, suppliers, and production services.
*Distribution*: 10,500.
*Rates*: Full-page color $1,450; full-page b&w $1,250.
*Reprints*: 1,000 color; 500 b&w.

*The Complete Annual Report and Corporate
Image Planning Book*
Alexander Communications, Inc.
212 West Superior Street #400
Chicago IL 60610
*Categories*: Design, illustration, photography, stock
photography, typography, printing, and paper.
*Distribution*: 15,000.
*Rates*: Full-page color $1,800; full-page b&w $1,600.
*Reprints*: 1,000.

*Corporate Showcase*
American Showcase
724 5th Avenue
New York NY 10019
(212) 245-0981
*Categories*: Illustrators, designers, and photographers
interested in corporate work. It is sent to corporations,
Fortune 1300 companies, public relations directors, and
promotions managers. It is released every August.
*Distribution*: Free distribution of 17,000 worldwide.
*Rates*: full-page color $3,000; full-page b&w $2,500.
*Reprints*: 2,000 free.

*Creative Black Book*
401 Park Avenue South
New York NY 10016
(212) 684-4255

*Categories*: One of the most frequently used creative talent directories, the *Creative Black Book* lists names, addresses, and phone numbers of illustrators, designers, and photographers. Volume I is for type, design, illustration, and TV, while Volume II is for photography.
*Distribution*: 40,000 worldwide. Free distribution includes art directors in large corporations, advertising agencies, and publishers.
*Rates*: Full-page color $6,175; full-page b&w $3,600.
*Reprints*: 2,000 free with color ads if first mechanical deadline is met.

### Creative Illustration
*Macmillan Creative Services Group*
*115 5th Avenue*
*New York NY 10003*
*(212) 254-1330*
*Categories*: Illustration and design. Also provides consultation services for portfolios and direct mail. Offers a flexible payment plan.
*Distribution*: 26,000 distributed to ad agencies, publishing houses, sales promotion firms, design studios, movie studios, and record companies.
*Rates*: Full-page color $2,215 if early deadline met; full-page b&w is $100 off of the color rates.
*Reprints*: 2,000 free with color ad.

### Directory of Illustration
*Graphic Artists Guild*
*Madison Square Press*
*10 East 23rd Street*
*New York NY 10010*
*(212) 475-1620*
*Categories*: 27 categories include humor, product, portrait, medical, science, transportation, science fiction, and sports.
*Distribution*: 22,000.
*Rates*: Full-page color $2,250; full-page b&w $150 less.
*Reprints*: 2,000 free.

### Madison Avenue Handbook
*17 East 48th Street*
*New York NY 10017*
*(212) 688-7940*
*Categories*: Performing talent, agencies, animation, film, video, photography, illustration, design, and printing.
*Distribution*: 25,000 to creative directors and public relations firms.
*Rates*: Full-page color $3,150; full-page b&w $2,150.
*Reprints*: 500 free for color ad.

### N. J. Source
*P.O. Box 640*
*Ramsey NJ 07446*
*(201) 825-0240*
*Categories*: Advertising, audiovisual, and broadcast media, graphic design and illustration, photography, printing, and other services.
*Distribution*: 15,000 issued; 12,000 to qualified art buyers.
*Rates*: Full-page color $2,450; full-page b&w $1,650.
*Reprints*: Provided at cost.

### N.Y. Gold
*150 5th Avenue*
*New York NY 10011*
*(212) 645-8022*
*Categories*: Design, illustration, humorous illustration, lettering, and photography.
*Distribution*: 13,000 free to ad agencies, corporations, and public relations firms.
*Rates*: Full-page color $2,700; full-page b&w is 10% off of the color rates.
*Reprints*: 2,000.

### RSVP
### The Directory of Creative Talent
*P.O. Box 314*
*Brooklyn NY 11205*
*(718) 857-9267*
*Categories*: This creative directory is known as a reasonably priced resource for illustrators, designers, photographers, and production artists.
*Distribution*: 15,000 to art directors at ad agencies, corporations, film studios, record companies, magazines, publishing houses, and government offices.
*Rates*: Full-page color $1,000-$1,500; full-page b&w $700-$1,000.
*Reprints*: 1,000.

### Texas Sourcebook
*Macmillan Creative Services Group*
*3102 Oaklawn #700*
*Dallas TX 75219*
*(214) 521-8066*
*Categories*: Illustration, design, photography, printing services, and video producers.
*Distribution*: 7,000 free copies distributed to ad agencies, design firms, and corporations.
*Rates*: Full-page color $1,650; full-page b&w $1,450.
*Reprints*: 500.

*The Workbook*
*Scott & Daughters Publishing*
*940 North Highland Avenue*
*Los Angeles CA 90038*
*(213) 856-0008*
*Categories*: *Illustration Portfolio* contains names of illustrators and designers; also publishes the *Photography Portfolio* and *Suppliers Directory*. The portfolios are nationwide in scope, while the supply directories are regional.
*Distribution*: 21,000 distributed free, 33,000 printed.
*Rates*: Full-page color $3,500; full-page b&w $2,400.
*Reprints*: 1,000.

*WorkSource*
*Turnbull & Co.*
*19 Mount Auburn Street*
*Cambridge MA 02138*
*(617) 864-1110*
*Categories*: Designers, illustrators, photographers, and production services in New England.
*Distribution*: 12,000 free to art buyers, ad agencies, corporations, and design firms.
*Rates*: Full-page color $1,460; full-page b&w $1,270.
*Reprints*: 1,000 free to buyers of one-half page or larger.

## LISTS

*Creative Access*
*415 West Superior*
*Chicago IL 60610*
*(312) 440-1140*
*(800) 422-2377*
Creative Access is a research firm providing sales support to the creative, production, design, and stock photography industries. Over 42,000 art buyers at ad agencies, corporations, and graphic design firms nationwide are listed. Creative Access also sells lists of illustrators, photographers, graphic designers, film directors, artist representatives, and production houses. Files are updated every four to six months through direct telephone interviews. Creative Access can provide names on pressure-sensitive labels, mag tape format, and Rolodex cards or in galley formats. It also has a research department which can provide research on a confidential basis.

*Steve Langerman Lists*
*437 Elmwood Avenue*
*Maplewood NJ 07040*
*(212) 466-3822*
*(201) 762-2786*
Steve Langerman sells art director listings for about eighteen major cities in the U.S. Categories include ad agencies, consumer magazines, public relations firms, cosmetic companies, and department stores. Write for a complete ordering kit.

# *Index*

# Improve your skills, learn a new technique, with these additional books from North Light

## Graphics/Business of Art

Airbrush Artist's Library (6 in series) $12.95 (cloth)
Airbrush Techniques Workbooks (8 in series) $9.95 each
Airbrushing the Human Form, by Andy Charlesworth $19.95 (cloth)
The Art & Craft of Greeting Cards, by Susan Evarts $15.95 (paper)
Artist's Market: Where & How to Sell Your Graphic Art (Annual Directory) $19.95 (cloth)
Basic Desktop Design & Layout, by Collier & Cotton $27.95 (cloth)
Basic Graphic Design & Paste-Up, by Jack Warren $13.95 (paper)
Business & Legal Forms for Graphic Designers, by Tad Crawford $19.95 (paper)
Business and Legal Forms for Illustrators, by Tad Crawford $15.95
CLICK: The Brightest in Computer-Generated Design and Illustration $39.95 (cloth)
COLORWORKS: The Designer's Ultimate Guide to Working with Color, by Dale Russell (5 in series) $24.95 ea.
Color Harmony: A Guide to Creative Color Combinations, by Hideaki Chijiiwa $15.95 (paper)
Complete Airbrush & Photoretouching Manual, by Peter Owen & John Sutcliffe $24.95 (cloth)
The Complete Guide to Greeting Card Design & Illustration, by Eva Szela $27.95 (cloth)
Creating Dynamic Roughs, by Alan Swann $27.95 (cloth)
Creative Director's Sourcebook, by Nick Souter and Stuart Neuman $89.00 (cloth)
Creative Typography, by Marion March $27.95 (cloth)
Design Rendering Techniques, by Dick Powell $29.95 (cloth)
Dynamic Airbrush, by David Miller & James Effler $29.95 (cloth)
Fantasy Art, by Bruce Robertson $24.95 (cloth)
Fashion Illustration Workbooks (4 in series) $8.95 each
59 More Studio Secrets, by Susan Davis $29.95 (cloth)
Getting It Printed, by Beach, Shepro & Russon $29.50 (paper)
Getting Started as a Freelance Illustrator or Designer, by Michael Fleischman $16.95 (paper)
Getting Started in Computer Graphics, by Gary Olsen $27.95 (paper)
The Graphic Artist's Guide to Marketing & Self-Promotion, by Sally Prince Davis $15.95 (paper)
The Graphic Designer's Basic Guide to the Macintosh, by Meyerowitz and Sanchez $19.95 (paper)
Graphics Handbook, by Howard Munce $14.95 (paper)
Handbook of Pricing & Ethical Guidelines, 7th edition, by The Graphic Artist's Guild $22.95 (paper)
Homage to the Alphabet: Typeface Sourcebook, $39.95 (cloth)
HOT AIR: An Explosive Collection of Top Airbrush Illustration, $39.95 (cloth)
How to Check and Correct Color Proofs, by David Bann $27.95 (cloth)
How to Design Trademarks & Logos, by Murphy & Row $24.95 (cloth)
How to Draw & Sell Cartoons, by Ross Thomson & Bill Hewison $18.95 (cloth)
How to Draw & Sell Comic Strips, by Alan McKenzie $18.95 (cloth)
How to Draw Charts & Diagrams, by Bruce Robertson $24.95 (cloth)
How to Find and Work with an Illustrator, by Martin Colyer $24.95 (cloth)

How to Understand & Use Design & Layout, by Alan Swann $19.95 (paper)
How to Understand & Use Grids, by Alan Swann $27.95 (cloth)
How to Write and Illustrate Children's Books, edited by Treld Pelkey Bicknell and Felicity Trotman, $22.50 (cloth)
Label Design 2, by Walker and Blount $49.95 (cloth)
Legal Guide for the Visual Artist, Revised Edition by Tad Crawford $18.95 (paper)
Letterhead & Logo Designs: Creating the Corporate Image $49.95 (cloth)
Licensing Art & Design, by Caryn Leland $12.95 (paper)
Living by Your Brush Alone, by Edna Wagner Piersol $16.95 (paper)
Make It Legal, by Lee Wilson $18.95 (paper)
Making Your Computer a Design & Business Partner, by Walker and Blount $27.95 (paper)
Marker Rendering Techniques, by Dick Powell & Patricia Monahan $32.95 (cloth)
Marker Techniques Workbooks (8 in series) $9.95 each
North Light Dictionary of Art Terms, by Margy Lee Elspass $12.95 (paper)
Preparing Your Design for Print, by Lynn John $27.95 (cloth)
Presentation Techniques for the Graphic Artist, by Jenny Mulherin $24.95 (cloth)
Primo Angeli: Designs for Marketing, $27.95 (paper)
Print Production Handbook, by David Bann $16.95 (cloth)
PROMO: The Ultimate in Graphic Designer's and Illustrator's Self-Promotion $39.95 (cloth)
Ready to Use Layouts for Desktop Design, by Chris Prior $27.95 (cloth)
Studio Secrets for the Graphic Artist, by Jack Buchan $29.95 (cloth)
Trademarks & Symbols of the World (three volumes) $24.95 ea. (paper)
Type & Color: A Handbook of Creative Combinations, by Cook and Fleury $34.95 (cloth)
Type: Design, Color, Character & Use, by Michael Beaumont $19.95 (paper)
Using Type Right, by Philip Brady $18.95 (paper)

## Watercolor

Big Brush Watercolor, by Ron Ranson $22.95 (cloth)
Chinese Watercolor Painting: The Four Seasons, by Leslie Tseng-Tseng Yu $24.95 (paper)
The Complete Watercolor Book, by Wendon Blake $29.95 (cloth)
Fill Your Watercolors with Light and Color, by Roland Roycraft $27.95 (cloth)
Flower Painting, by Paul Riley $27.95 (cloth)
Getting Started in Watercolor, by John Blockley $19.95 (paper)
The New Spirit of Watercolor, by Mike Ward $27.95 (cloth)
Painting Nature's Details in Watercolor, by Cathy Johnson $19.95 (paper)
Painting Watercolor Portraits That Glow, by Jan Kunz $27.95 (cloth)
Sir William Russell Flint, edited by Ralph Lewis & Keith Gardner $55.00 (cloth)
Starting with Watercolor, by Rowland Hilder $24.95 (cloth)
Tony Couch Watercolor Techniques Workbook 1 & 2, by Tony Couch $12.95 each (paper)
Watercolor Impressionists, edited by Ron Ranson $45.00

Watercolor Painter's Solution Book, by Angela Gair $24.95 (cloth)

Watercolor: Painting Smart, by Al Stine $27.95 (cloth)

Watercolor – The Creative Experience, by Barbara Nechis $16.95 (paper)

Watercolor Tricks & Techniques, by Cathy Johnson $24.95 (cloth)

Watercolor Workbook, by Bud Biggs & Lois Marshall $19.95 (paper)

Watercolor: You Can Do It!, by Tony Couch $26.95 (cloth)

Webb on Watercolor, by Frank Webb $29.95 (cloth)

## Watercolor Videos

Big Brush Watercolor, with Ron Ranson $29.95 (VHS only)

Watercolor Fast & Loose, with Ron Ranson $29.95 (VHS or Beta)

Watercolor Pure & Simple, with Ron Ranson $29.95 (VHS or Beta)

## Mixed Media

The Art of Scratchboard, by Cecile Curtis $23.95 (cloth)

The Artist's Complete Health & Safety Guide, by Monona Rossol $16.95 (paper)

Blue and Yellow Don't Make Green, by Michael Wilcox $24.95 (cloth)

Bodyworks: A Visual Guide to Drawing the Figure, by Marbury Hill Brown $24.95 (cloth)

Business & Legal Forms for Fine Artists, by Tad Crawford $12.95 (paper)

Calligraphy Workbooks (4 in series) $7.95 each

Colored Pencil Drawing Techniques, by Iain Hutton-Jamieson $24.95 (cloth)

The Complete Acrylic Painting Book, by Wendon Blake $29.95 (cloth)

The Complete Guide to Screenprinting, by Brad Faine $24.95 (cloth)

Complete Guide to Fashion Illustration, by Colin Barnes $32.95 (cloth)

The Complete Oil Painting Book, by Wendon Blake $29.95 (cloth)

The Creative Artist, by Nita Leland $27.95 (cloth)

Creative Basketmaking, by Lois Walpole $24.95 (cloth)

Creative Painting with Pastel, by Carole Katchen $27.95 (cloth)

Decorative Painting for Children's Rooms, by Rosie Fisher $29.95 (cloth)

Drawing & Painting Animals, by Cecile Curtis $26.95 (cloth)

Drawing Workbooks (4 in series) $8.95 each

Dynamic Color Drawing, by Judy Martin $26.95 (cloth)

Exploring Color, by Nita Leland $19.95 (paper)

The Figure, edited by Walt Reed $16.95 (paper)

Fine Artist's Guide to Showing & Selling Your Work, by Sally Price Davis $16.95 (paper)

The Half Hour Painter, by Alwyn Crawshaw $18.95 (paper)

Handtinting Photographs, by Martin and Colbeck $28.95 (cloth)

How to Paint Living Portraits, by Roberta Carter Clark $27.95 (cloth)

Introduction to Batik, by Griffin & Holmes $9.95 (paper)

Keys to Drawing, by Bert Dodson $19.95 (paper)

Light: How to See It, How to Paint It, by Lucy Willis $24.95 (cloth)

Make Your Own Picture Frames, by Jenny Rodwell $12.95 (paper)

Mixing Color, by Jeremy Galton $24.95 (cloth)

The North Light Handbook of Artist's Materials, by Ian Hebblewhite $24.95 (cloth)

The North Light Illustrated Book of Painting Techniques, by Elizabeth Tate $27.95 (cloth)

Oil Painting: A Direct Approach, by Joyce Pike $26.95 (cloth)

Painting Birds & Animals, by Patricia Monahan $21.95 (cloth)

Painting Floral Still Lifes, by Joyce Pike $19.95 (paper)

Painting in Mixed Media, by Moira Huntly $23.95 (paper)

Painting More Than the Eye Can See, by Robert Wade $29.95 (cloth)

Painting Seascapes in Sharp Focus, by Lin Seslar $19.95 (paper)

Painting with Acrylics, by Jenny Rodwell $19.95 (paper)

Painting with Oils, by Patricia Monahan $19.95 (cloth)

Painting with Pastels, edited by Peter D. Johnson $16.95 (paper)

Pastel Painting Techniques, by Guy Roddon $24.95 (cloth)

The Pencil, by Paul Calle $17.95 (paper)

People Painting Scrapbook, by J. Everett Draper $26.95 (cloth)

Perspective in Art, by Michael Woods $13.95 (paper)

Perspective Without Pain Workbooks (4 in series) $9.95 each

Photographing Your Artwork, by Russell Hart $16.95 (paper)

Tonal Values: How to See Them, How to Paint Them, by Angela Gair $24.95 (cloth)

To order directly from the publisher, include $3.00 postage and handling for one book, $1.00 for each additional book. Allow 30 days for delivery.

North Light Books
1507 Dana Avenue, Cincinnati, Ohio 45207
Credit card orders
Call TOLL-FREE
1-800-289-0963
Prices subject to change without notice.